Explode The Code®

Teacher's Guide for Books 5 and 6

Nancy Hall

Explode The Code® 5
Essential lessons for phonics mastery
Nancy Hall • Rena Price

Explode The Code® 6
Essential lessons for phonics mastery
Nancy Hall • Rena Price

out

law

outlaw

School Specialty, Inc.

Cambridge and Toronto

Acquisitions/Development: Sethany Rancier Alongi
Editor: Elissa Gershowitz
Cover Design: David Parra
Typesetting: Kathleen Richards
Managing Editor: Sheila Neylon

Printed in Benton Harbor, MI, in May 2011
ISBN 978-0-8388-0855-9

7 8 9 PPG 13 12 11

Introduction

The No Child Left Behind Act of 2001 mandates that states formulate reading standards for each grade with the goal of having all children reading proficiently by the end of third grade. Federal money, through Reading First funds, will be available to help achieve these goals for states adopting reading programs in which the early reading skills of phonemic awareness, phonics, fluency, vocabulary, and comprehension are systematically and explicitly taught. *Explode The Code*® meets these standards.

Systematic, Direct Teaching of Phonics

Jeanne Chall's *Learning to Read: The Great Debate*—an extensive review of classroom, laboratory, and clinical research—revealed the efficacy of a direct, explicit, systematic teaching of decoding skills. Chall concluded that code emphasis programs produced better results, "not only in terms of the mechanical aspects of literacy alone, as was once supposed, but also in terms of the ultimate goals of reading instruction—comprehension and possibly even speed of reading" (Chall 1967, 307).

Even as new understandings about learning and teaching have evolved in the years since 1967, these findings have been repeatedly reconfirmed (Bond and Dykstra 1967; Chall 1983; Adams 1990; National Reading Panel 2000). In 2000, the National Reading Panel presented its findings of studies comparing phonics instruction with other kinds of instruction, published since 1970. Focusing on kindergarten through sixth grade, the panel concluded that systematic phonics instruction enhanced children's ability to read, spell, and comprehend text, particularly in the younger grades. These results were especially evident in the word-reading skills of disabled readers and low socioeconomic children, and for the spelling skills of good readers.

Chall and Popp write of "two kinds of meaning—meaning of the medium (the print) and the meaning of the message (the ideas)" (1996, 2). Knowledge of phonics gives students the ability to decode print, which in turn reveals the message ideas. The more words early readers can recognize, the more accessible meaning becomes. Children who have difficulty identifying words lack the fluency needed to concentrate on meaning (Rasinsky 2000). Conversely, children who are given direct, systematic instruction in decoding skills have the tools for developing fluent, meaningful reading. Furthermore, they have the tools to produce print and consequently express their thoughts in writing, which in turn reinforces their word identification skills (Ehri 1998).

Explode The Code offers a complete systematic phonics program for the elementary grades. Phonetic elements and patterns, carefully sequenced to consider both frequency of use and difficulty, are presented in sequence and practiced in a series of instructive workbooks. Teacher's Guides and Keys accompany all the books.

The first three books in the *Explode The Code* series—Books A, B, and C—focus on visual identification of consonants, their written lowercase letter forms, and their sound–symbol relationships. An engaging, colorful wall chart with felt objects representing key words for the twenty-six letters of the alphabet may be used to introduce children to the names and sounds of the lowercase letters and/or to reinforce lessons in books A, B, and C. An activity book with instructions for thirty-five games comes with the wall chart. Key word picture–letter cards are also provided.

The remaining eight books—*Explode The Code* Books 1–8—progress through the vowel sounds and patterns, consonant clusters and digraphs, syllables, and suffixes. Posttests are found at the end of each workbook. If extra practice is needed, an additional workbook for reinforcement accompanies each of books 1–6. Code Cards reinforce and review the letter sounds taught in *Explode The Code* Books 1–3½.

Through systematic direct teaching of phonics using *Explode The Code,* the following successes in reading and writing occur:

- The alphabetic principle is firmly established.
- Phonological awareness skills are fostered alongside the phonics teaching.
- Understanding of how sound–symbol relationships permit words and text to be decoded and encoded is fully developed and practiced, enhancing fluency and automaticity.
- Students of varying language and skill need are accommodated through vocabulary and concept building, exposure to differing approaches to teaching phonics, and flexible grouping and use of the materials.
- See more about the research for this series at http://www.epsbooks.com.

References

Adams, M. J. (1990). *Beginning to Read: Thinking and Learning about Print.* Cambridge, MA: MIT Press.

Bond, G. & Dykstra, R. (1967). "The cooperative research program in first grade reading." *Reading Research Quarterly* 2: 5-142.

Chall, J. S. (1967, 1983). *Learning to Read: The Great Debate.* New York: McGraw Hill.

Chall, J. S. & Popp, H. M. (1996). *Teaching and Assessing Phonics, Why, What, When, How: A Guide for Teachers.* Cambridge, MA: Educators Publishing Service.

Ehri, L. C. (1998). "Grapheme-phoneme knowledge is essential for learning to read words in English." In: Metsala, J. L. & Ehri, L. C. (eds.) *Word Recognition in Beginning Literacy.* Mahwah, NJ: Erlbaum, 3-40.

National Reading Panel (2000). *Teaching Children to Read: An Evidence Based Assessment of the Scientific Research Literature on Reading and Its Implication for Reading Instruction: Reports of the Subgroups.* Washington: National Institute of Child Health and Development.

Rasinsky, T. V. (2000). "Does speed matter in reading?" *The Reading Teacher* 54:146-151.

Explode The Code Books 5 and 6 Teacher's Guide and Key

Explode The Code Teacher's Guides expand on the skills presented in the student books, providing teachers with various options for instruction and reinforcement. The guides address the principles of phonemic awareness, phonics, vocabulary, fluency, and comprehension as they relate to each new skill presented in the lesson. They also include suggestions for writing practice and differentiating instruction. Each lesson follows the same easy-to-use format:

Link to Prior Knowledge/Quick Review   Each new lesson begins by helping students make connections to previously learned concepts or sound–symbol relationships.

Phonological/Phonemic Awareness   This section provides instruction to help students recognize and manipulate the sounds in spoken words. Struggling learners may need this kind of support on an ongoing basis in order to improve their ability to read and spell. The oral activities in this section help students focus in on and work with the sounds of words in the lesson. The activities include the following: blending and segmentation; discriminating and matching sounds in words; substituting sounds in words to create new words; identifying rhymes.

Phonics   This section helps students learn the sound–symbol relationships necessary for decoding words. Teachers introduce each skill by calling attention to sounds in familiar words. Then they teach students the letter or letters that represent that sound. Students then practice the skill, working with other words that include that phonic element.

Vocabulary   Learning new words is essential to the development of reading comprehension. This section defines unfamiliar words from the lesson. It also identifies direction words and sight words necessary for completing the exercises.

Completing Student Pages   This section directs the class to the corresponding *Explode The Code* student books. Teachers read the student book directions with the class and check for understanding of the task. They identify any unfamiliar illustrations and walk through a sample item on each page. Each student book lesson follows a predictable format; as students learn the format, they should be able to complete the pages without further assistance.

Comprehension   In order for students to fully understand what they read, they need to be able to use, discuss, define, and understand words in a variety of ways. The comprehension-building activities in this section expand students' understanding of lesson words and concepts by having them answer questions, work with synonyms and antonyms, use words in oral sentences, draw pictures, work with parts of speech and word endings, and complete riddles or other word games. Students can then apply their word comprehension skills to a variety of texts.

Fluency   Fluent readers spend less time decoding words and give more attention to comprehending text. In this section, a variety of fluency activities help students develop skills in reading sentences and passages accurately and quickly. The rotating menu of fluency-building activities includes the following: noting punctuation, developing or improving accuracy, reading with expression, articulation, reading dialogue, varying pitch and volume, improving rate, syllable stress, and phrasing.

Writing   Writing goes hand-in-hand with phonics instruction. In this section, students are asked to incorporate words from the lesson as they write word clues, sentences, similes, tongue twisters, riddles, poems, book reports, and stories.

Differentiating Instruction   The rotating menu of activities in this section provides suggestions accommodating a broad range of learning needs and styles. **ELL** tips and activities help teachers identify and accommodate potential problem areas for English-language learners. **Extra Practice** refers teachers to lessons in Books 5½ and 6½ that can be used for extra practice. **Challenge** activities are provided for students who complete the student book pages without difficulty. **Learning Styles** activities address the learning styles of kinesthetic, visual/spatial, auditory, musical, or linguistic learners. **Computer-based Reinforcement** activities direct teachers to *ETC Online,* where students can get additional practice with *Explode The Code* phonics skills in an interactive, dynamic format.

Key   Answers to the posttests for Books 5, 5½, 6, and 6½ are provided.

Explode The Code Coordinating Materials

Explode The Code **Placement Test**   The tests in this quick assessment help teachers determine student placement within the *Explode The Code* series.

Ready, Set, Go **Picture–Letter Cards**   *Ready, Set, Go* Picture–Letter Cards feature initial consonants taught in Books A, B, and C. The set consists of twenty sheets, each with a picture card, a letter card, and a picture card with the letter superimposed.

Wall Chart and Activity Book   The *Explode The Code* Wall Chart is a colorful felt wall chart with letter pockets containing tangible felt objects that reinforce the key words for the twenty-six letters of the alphabet and their sounds. The Activity Book for the Wall Chart provides ideas for several activities and games to further aid in learning the names and sounds of the letters taught in Books A, B, C, and 1.

Explode The Code **Code Cards**   This set of fifty-four index cards reinforces the sound–symbol relationships taught in *Explode The Code* Books 1–3. Code Cards can be used for instruction and review.

Explode The Code for English Language Learners   This resource supplements instruction of *Explode The Code* Books 1–3 by providing specific direction for teachers of English-language learners. Reproducible student pages are included.

Explode The Code **Extra Practice Books**   *Explode The Code* Books 1½–6½ provide further practice in the skills taught in Books 1–6.

Beyond The Code   The *Beyond The Code* books provide opportunities for advanced reading of longer stories. These books incorporate skills from the *Explode The Code* books, introduce many more sight words, and emphasize reading comprehension and critical thinking.

ETC Online   *ETC Online* presents the *Explode The Code* content in an interactive and dynamic format. *ETC Online's* adaptive technology adjusts the content it delivers automatically, according to the student's performance. It has extensive feedback features for students, parents, teachers, and administrators. See www.explodethecode.com for details.

Book 5

Lesson 1
-*ed* words (/ĕd/)

Link to Prior Knowledge

Review syllable division rules from Book 4, including vc/cv, v/cv, vc/v. Ask volunteers to divide words into syllables, explain the rule they used, and read the words: *napkin (nap/kin; vc/cv), halo (ha/lo; v/cv), robin (rob/in; vc/v), raisin (rai/sin; v/cv), sample (sam/ple; -le at the end of words takes the consonant before it to make the last syllable), twenty (twen/ty; y says /ē/ and takes the consonant before it to make the last syllable).*

In Lesson 2 of Book 4, students learned that adding certain endings to words can make new words. The ending -*ed* is one example. Review what an action word is. Tell students that if you add the ending -*ed* to most action words, it means the action has already happened. Then tell students that when -*ed* is added to a word ending in *d* or *t*, it says /ĕd/. Tell students that this lesson is about action words that end with /ĕd/.

Phonemic Awareness

Discriminating Sounds   Ask students to listen as you say several words. Have them clap their hands each time they hear a word that ends with /ĕd/.

pointed (clap)   hire
limited (clap)   tended (clap)
barking   leaping

Phonics

Introduce the Skill   Tell students that many words end with the letters -*ed*, but in this lesson, they will only be reading and writing words in which the -*ed* says /ĕd/.

Write the following words on the board: *elect, plant, braid, brand, rest.* Say each word slowly. Then ask volunteers to circle the final *d* or *t* in each word, add the -*ed* ending, and say the new words (*elected, planted, braided, branded, rested*).

Ask each student to think of three other action words that end with *d* or *t*. Have them list the words on a piece of paper and add -*ed* to each word. Ask students to share their lists with a neighbor. When everyone is finished sharing, ask volunteers to name some of the words on their list and add them to the list on the board.

Vocabulary

Introduce New Vocabulary   If you are not sure that students are familiar with certain lesson words or concepts, provide explanations. For example, if you're **spattered** with mud, you have it all over your clothes. If someone **boasted** about his talent, he has spoken about himself with pride, but may have exaggerated his skills.

Introduce Sight Words   Introduce the new sight words used in the lesson: *all, your, have, could, would, are, wild, were, very,* and *they.* Have students make up sentences using each word. Then ask the class to repeat the sight words and spell them aloud. Have them write the letters in the air using their fingers as a pencil. Add these words to the Word Wall or have students add them to their personal dictionaries.

Introduce Direction Words   The words *words, usually, something, already, write, using, sentence, sound, done, first, root,* and *says* are used in the directions for this book. If you want students to learn to read these words, introduce them the same way you introduce the sight words.

Completing Student Pages 1–8

Identify any pictures that may be unfamiliar to students, such as *harp* in item 2 and *explode* in item 5 on page 1. Together, read the directions and work through the sample item on each page. Then direct students to complete the pages independently, providing assistance as needed.

Fluency

Varying Pitch and Volume   Have partners pick a sentence from page 4 and practice reading it with expression. For example, sentence 6 includes the word *tremble.* Demonstrate saying the word in a way that conveys its meaning.

Comprehension

Ask students to draw a picture that illustrates one of the following words: *twisted, fainted, inspected, demanded.* Have students label their pictures with the word, and share with the class the reasons they drew the picture they did.

Writing   Write the following words on the board: *landed, nested, frosted, added, rested, hunted, spattered.* Divide the class into groups and ask each group to write a sentence that uses at least two of the words. Encourage students to write more descriptive sentences by having them give information about where or when something happened. For example: *After he **frosted** the cake* (when), *Dad **rested** in his chair* (where) *until dinnertime* (when). Ask groups to share their sentences with the class.

Differentiating Instruction

Extra Practice   For extra practice with /ĕd/, have students complete the activities in *Explode The Code* Book 5½, Lesson 8.

Learning Styles (Visual/Kinesthetic)   Write ten action words that end with *d* or *t* on index cards. On another card, write *ed.* Spread out all the cards on a table. Have students move the *ed* card next to each action card to make words that end with /ĕd/. Then have them read the words aloud or silently.

ELL   Some students who speak Asian languages, in particular, may have difficulty with the *-ed* ending. Make sure students recognize the difference between the present and past tenses of the action words, and use them correctly. Write a sentence such as the following on the board: *Lin **rest/rested** after her long flight home.* Ask students to read the sentence aloud and choose the correct form of the action word *rest*.

Computer-based Reinforcement   Give students additional practice with *-ed* words on *ETC Online*, Units 5.1.2 to 5.1.7.

Lesson 2
-ed words (/d/, /t/)

Link to Prior Knowledge
Ask students if they remember what happens when action words with final *d* and *t* have the *-ed* ending added to them. (The *-ed* is said /ĕd/.) Ask students to provide examples (*elected, planted, braided, branded, rested*). Tell students that when the *-ed* ending is added to action words that do not end in *d* or *t,* the *-ed* ending sounds like /t/ or /d/, as in *rocked* (/t/) or *mowed* (/d/). Tell students that this lesson is about these *-ed* words that say /d/ and /t/ at the end.

Phonemic Awareness
Discriminating Sounds   Say the following words slowly and ask students whether they hear /d/ or /t/ at the end of each: *clapped* (/t/), *tricked* (/t/), *spelled* (/t/ or /d/), *stained* (/d/), *mowed* (/d/), *jumped* (/t/).

Phonics
Introduce the Skill   Write on the board the words *fix* and *play*. Ask students what ending you add to an action word to show that something has already happened. Write *-ed* at the end of *fix*, and ask students to read it and use the word in a sentence. Ask what sound *-ed* makes at the end of *fixed* (/t/). Repeat the exercise, changing *play* to *played*. Ask what sound *-ed* makes this time (/d/). Have students use *played* in a sentence. Continue using other action words that end with /d/ and /t/ after adding the *-ed* ending.

Vocabulary
Introduce New Vocabulary   If you are not sure whether students are familiar with certain lesson words or concepts, provide explanations. For example, a **leaky** faucet will keep dripping water unless it is **fixed**. A **hammock** is something you lie on to feel **relaxed**, that's made of rope and strung between two trees or poles. If a rope is being **yanked** by two

people, they are quickly pulling it in opposite directions. If someone **dashed** away it means they quickly went somewhere else. If something **vanished** the object has disappeared.

Introduce Sight Words   Introduce the new sight words used in the lesson: *one, pull,* and *was.* Have students make up sentences using the words. Then ask the class to repeat the sight words and spell them aloud. Have them write the letters in the air using their fingers as a pencil. Add these words to the Word Wall or have students add them to their personal dictionaries.

Completing Student Pages 9–16

Identify any pictures that may be unfamiliar to students, such as *fern* in item 5 and *all* in item 6 on page 9. Together, read the directions and work through the first item on each page. Then direct students to complete the pages independently, providing assistance as needed.

Fluency

Partner Reading   Have students take turns rereading the sentences on pages 12, 14, and 15 with the person sitting next to them. Instruct students to monitor each other for accuracy and expression.

Comprehension

Write on the board some sentences with fill-in-the-blank choices for the action words. For example, write: *Yesterday, Juan* **plays/played/playing** *basketball with his friends.* Have students decide which form of the action word is correct and tell why.

Writing   Have students write a short story about a real or imaginary fishing trip, using as many action words ending with *-ed* as they can. Remind them to make sure their stories can answer the questions *who? where? when?* and *what happened?*

Differentiating Instruction
Extra Practice   For extra practice with *-ed* as /t/ and /d/, have students complete the activities in *Explode The Code* Book 5½, Lessons 9 and 10.

ELL   Children might have difficulty understanding some of the action words in the lesson. Whenever possible, pantomime actions yourself or ask for volunteers.

Challenge   For students who complete these pages without difficulty, write the following words on the board: *adopted, boiled, shredded, cheated, stamped, framed, greeted, swelled, tricked, possessed, increased.* On a piece of paper have each student make a three-column chart, labeled /ĕd/, /t/, /d/. They should then say the words on the board, listening for the *ed, t,* or *d* sound at the end, and write each word in the appropriate column.

Computer-based Reinforcement   Give students additional practice with *-ed* words on *ETC Online,* Units 5.2.2 to 5.2.7.

Lesson 3
-*all* and -*alk* words

Link to Prior Knowledge

Ask students what sound the letter *a* makes in short vowel words like *bat, tag,* and *tack* (/ă/). Then ask what sound it makes in long vowel words like *cake, date, pail, nail, play,* and *say* (/ā/). Explain to students that when you add the letters *ll* or *lk* after a short *a*, it changes the *a* sound in that word. Tell students that this lesson is about words spelled with -*all* and -*alk*.

Phonemic Awareness

Matching Sounds   Tell students that some word families have special sounds. Say the words *ball* and *walk*. The -*all* and -*alk* word families make the sound /aw/, as in *ball* and *walk*. Have students listen to the following clues and name the word being described in each. Then ask whether the word belongs in the same word family as *ball* or *walk*.

> This word starts like /ch/ and is used to write on the board in school. (*chalk; "walk" word family*)
>
> This word starts like /k/ and is what you do when you use the telephone. (*call; "ball" word family*)
>
> This word starts like /h/ and is what you walk down to get to class. (*hall; "ball" word family*)
>
> This words starts like /t/ and means *speak*. (*talk; "walk" word family*)
>
> This word starts like /sm/ and means *little*. (*small; "ball" word family*)
>
> This word starts like /f/ and is the name of one of the seasons (*fall; "ball" word family*)

Phonics

Introduce the Skill   Explain to students that sometimes the *aw* sound is spelled *all* or *alk* in words. Tell them that they will be reading and writing some of these words in this lesson.

Ask volunteers to think of other words that rhyme with *ball* (*mall, tall, wall, fall, stall, hall*) and *chalk* (*walk, talk, stalk*). Write the words in columns on the board and have students read them aloud with you. Then ask volunteers to circle the letters in each word that say /aw/.

Vocabulary

Introduce New Vocabulary   If you are not sure whether students are familiar with certain lesson words or concepts, provide explanations. For example, a horse lives in a **stall** in the barn. If a group of people is **ailing**, they **all** don't feel well. The long, green stem of a plant is also called a **stalk**. A **tall tale** is a silly story about a hero. To **recall** is to remember something.

Introduce Sight Words   Introduce the new sight word used in the lesson: *who.* Have students make up sentences using the word. Then ask the class to repeat the sight word and spell it aloud. Have them write the letters in the air using their fingers as a pencil. Add the word to the Word Wall or have students add it to their personal dictionaries.

Completing Student Pages 17–24

Identify any pictures that may be unfamiliar to students, such as *target* in item 1 on page 17. Together, read the directions and then direct students to complete the pages independently, providing assistance as needed.

Fluency

Articulation   Have students practice articulating all the sounds in *-all* and *-alk* words by rereading sentences on pages 20 and 22. Walk around the room, listening to pairs and monitoring for correct articulation.

Repeated Reading   Direct students to page 35 of "Kal Grows Up and Up" from *Beyond The Code* Book 3. Model reading aloud while the class follows along. Then assign partners and have them take turns reading it to each other. Finally, ask students to read it in unison. Remind them to use appropriate expression when they encounter commas, semicolons, and exclamation points, and to emphasize boldface words, as necessary.

Comprehension

Extending Word Knowledge   Write the word *talk* on the board. Ask students to think of other words that describe how someone might communicate; for example: *shout.* Write these words on the board. Do the same for the word *walk.*

Writing   Ask students to choose three *-all* words from the lesson and write one sentence using all of them; repeat with *-alk* words. When everyone has finished writing, ask volunteers to share their sentences with the class. Examples: *Kick the **ball** to the **tall wall**. I will **walk** holding **chalk** while I **talk** to my teacher.*

Differentiating Instruction
Extra Practice   For extra practice with *-all* and *-alk* words, have students complete the activities in *Explode The Code* Book 5½, Lesson 1.

Challenge   Have students who complete these pages without difficulty make up their own clues for five *-all* or *-alk* words from the lesson. For example: *This is a season when leaves come off the trees* (fall).

Computer-based Reinforcement   Give students additional practice with *-all* and *-alk* words on *ETC Online,* Units 5.3.2 to 5.3.7.

Lesson 4
-old, -olt, and -oll words

Link to Prior Knowledge

Ask students what the vowel o says at the end of a little word like go (/ō/). Then ask what it says in silent e words like hope, wrote, and stone (/ō/). Have students name some additional long o words. Tell them that this lesson is about word families with long o, spelled -olt, -oll, and -old, as in cold.

Phonemic Awareness

Word Rhyming   Tell students you are going to say sets of three words and you want them to listen to how the words end. After each set of words, ask which two sound alike at the end.

bold, sold, tell (bold, sold)	trip, troll, toll (toll, troll)
roll, ball, stroll (roll, stroll)	gold, melt, fold (gold, fold)
dealt, bolt, colt (bolt, colt)	lull, mold, hold (mold, hold)

Phonics

Introduce the Skill   Have students repeat the following words: colt, fold, roll. Ask what these three words have in common. Point out that each has a long o sound that comes before the consonant l. Tell students that in this lesson they will be reading and writing words in the -old, -olt, and -oll word families.

Draw a three-column chart on the board labeled -old, -olt, and -oll, and have students make their own on a piece of paper. Then say the following words and have students write each word in the column in which it belongs.

told	sold
jolt	enroll
poll	revolt

Vocabulary

Introduce New Vocabulary   If you are not sure whether students are familiar with certain lesson words or concepts, provide explanations. For example, if your **colt** is **bucking**, it's jumping up and trying to throw you off its back. If a door is **bolted** shut, it is fastened with a bar of wood or metal. If you go over a bump and are bounced around you might feel **jolted**. If you **molded** a design out of clay or sand, you have shaped it to hold its form. A **colt** is a young male horse.

Introduce Sight Words   Introduce the new sight words used in the lesson: love, loved, live, lived, give. Have students make up sentences using each word. Then ask the class to repeat the sight words and spell them aloud. Have them write the letters in the air using their fingers as a pencil. Add these words to the Word Wall or have students add them to their personal dictionaries.

Completing Student Pages 25–32

Identify any pictures that may be unfamiliar to students, such as *handful* in item 1 and *stalk* in item 7 on page 25. Together, read the directions and direct students to complete the pages independently, providing assistance as needed.

Fluency

Developing Accuracy   Write the following words on the board. Read them aloud and have students repeat them: *molded, beach, colt, saddle, scolded, rattlesnake, snowman, trunk, bolted, bubbles, tumble, bucking, jolted.* Have students repeat the words one more time. Then have them pair off and practice reading the words to each other over and over again, until they can read the words smoothly without any errors or hesitations.

Comprehension

Read the following sentences aloud to the class. Ask students to fill in the blanks with an *-old, -olt,* or *-oll* word.

> I like to put butter and jam on my *blank.* (roll)
> My dad had to put in a new *blank* on the front door lock. (bolt)
> The car stopped short with a bump and a *blank.* (jolt)
> We *blank* our old car and bought a new one. (sold)
> I bought a silver and *blank* bracelet for my mom's birthday. (gold)

Writing   Provide students with the following story starters and ask them to write a short story. Encourage them to use as many *-old, -olt,* and *-oll* words as they can.

> On a **cold** day, I . . .
> My ball **rolled** into . . .
> The small **colt strolled** in the . . .

Differentiating Instruction

Extra Practice   For extra practice with *-old, -olt,* and *-oll* words, have students complete the activities in *Explode The Code* Book 5½, Lesson 2.

ELL   Since /l/ and /r/ are sometimes confused in Asian languages in particular, some students might have difficulty pronouncing words with *-old, -olt,* and *-oll.* Help students say the words in this lesson slowly, demonstrating where they should put their tongues in order to make the *l* sound.

Computer-based Reinforcement   Give students additional practice with *-olt, -olt,* and *-oll* words on *ETC Online,* Units 5.4.2 to 5.4.7.

Lesson 5
-ild and *-ind* words

Link to Prior Knowledge

In previous books, students learned about words with the long *i* sound. Ask them what the vowel *i* says at the end of a little word like *hi* (/ī/). Then ask them what the vowel *i* says in silent *e* words, as in *like, bite,* and *mine* (/ī/). Ask students to name some additional long *i* words. Tell them that this lesson is about long *i* word families: *-ild* as in *wild* and *-ind* as in *find.*

Phonemic Awareness

Sound Matching   Ask students to listen as you say several words. Have them clap each time they hear the long *i* sound.

mitt	blend
child (clap)	blind (clap)
mild (clap)	chilled
mint	mind (clap)

Phonics

Introduce the Skill   Tell students that the long *i* sound can be heard in many words, but in this lesson, they will be reading and writing words in the *-ild* and *-ind* word families.

Ask students to make a two-column chart on a piece of paper. They should head one column *-ild* and the other column *-ind.* Then ask them to write as many words in each column as they can in five minutes. When time is up, ask volunteers to call out their words as you write them on the board.

Vocabulary

Introduce New Vocabulary   If you are not sure whether students are familiar with certain lesson words or concepts, provide explanations. For example, the **rind** is the tough outer coating of some fruits. Something **mild** is calming and gentle. If you are **blinded** by something it means you can't see because of it.

Introduce Sight Words   Introduce the new sight words used in the lesson: *does* and *brother.* Have students make up sentences using each word. Then ask the class to repeat the sight words and spell them aloud. Have them write the letters in the air using their fingers as a pencil. Add these words to the Word Wall or have students add the words to their personal dictionaries.

Completing Student Pages 33–40

Identify any pictures that may be unfamiliar to students, such as *find* in item 1, *measles* and *mind* in item 6, and *world* in item 7 on page 33. Together, read the directions and then direct students to complete the pages independently, providing assistance as needed.

Fluency

Read with Expression   Assign partners and have students practice reading the sentences on page 36. They should take turns reading with expression, using their voices to indicate that they are asking a question.

Repeated Reading   Have students read page 10 of "Kids Need Pets" from *Beyond The Code* Book 3 to themselves. Model reading aloud while the class follows along. Then assign partners and have them take turns reading to each other. Finally, ask students to read it in unison. Remind them to use appropriate expression when they encounter commas, semicolons, and exclamation points, and to emphasize boldface words, as necessary.

Comprehension

Extending Word Knowledge   Write these words on the board: *wild, find, kind, child, behind, mild.* Ask volunteers to name an antonym, or opposite, of each word, and write them on the board (examples: *tame, lose, mean, adult, in front, rough*).

Writing   Ask students to write a sentence or short poem using two *-ind* words and two *-ild* words. Provide them with an example: *I will **find** a **kind** dog for that **wild child**.*

Differentiating Instruction

Extra Practice   For extra practice with *-ild* and *-ind* word families, have students complete the activities in *Explode The Code* Book 5½, Lesson 3.

Learning Styles (Kinesthetic)   Write *-ild* and *-ind* words on index cards and have students sort the cards by word family. Then ask students to copy each word on a separate index card for future reference.

Challenge   Have students who complete these pages without difficulty unscramble the following letters to make *-ild* and *-ind* words:

s i t l w d e (wildest)   h l i c s i d h (childish)

d i m r n e (remind)   i n r g i d g n (grinding)

n u i w d p (windup)

Computer-based Reinforcement   Give students additional practice with *-ild* and *-ind* words on *ETC Online*, Units 5.5.3 to 5.5.7.

Lesson 6
Review Lesson

Cumulative Review

Remind students that word families have their own special sounds. Ask if they remember the word families they have learned so far in *Explode The Code* Book 5. Write them on the board as column heads: *-all, -alk, -old, -olt, -oll, -ild, -ind.* Ask volunteers to think of a word for each family, and write them on the board under the corresponding word family. Tell students that this lesson will review these word families.

Phonemic Awareness

Matching Sounds   Remind students to think of the word families *-all, -alk, -old, -olt, -oll, -ild,* and *-ind,* and *-ed* words while doing this exercise. Ask students to listen to the following clues and then name the word described.

It starts like /m/ and is what happened to the snowman when the sun came out. (melted)
It starts like /k/ and is a young horse. (colt)
It starts like /ch/ and is another word for "kid." (child)
It starts like /m/ and is what a gardener did when the grass got too long. (mowed)
It starts like /b/ and is used in a sport played on a diamond. (baseball)
It starts like /w/ and tells what you did if you didn't drive or take the bus to school. (walked)

Phonics

Skill Review   Tell students that in this review lesson, they will be reading and writing words in the word families *-all, -alk, -old, -olt, -oll, -ild, -ind.*

Coordinate a spelling bee. Have students line up alphabetically by first name. Say a word from the *-all, -alk, -old, -olt, -oll, -ild,* or *-ind* word families, and ask the first student to spell the word. If it is spelled correctly, he or she goes to the end of the line and continues to play. If he or she spells incorrectly, the student sits down. The last student standing wins the spelling bee.

Vocabulary

Introduce New Vocabulary   If you are not sure whether students are familiar with certain lesson words or concepts, provide explanations. For example, if you **postpone** something, you delay doing it. If your **colt** is **frisky**, it is full of energy and likes to play. If you are being **scolded** by a teacher, that teacher is speaking harshly to punish you. **Bleachers** are outdoor seats you sit on to watch a game like baseball, football, or soccer. A **grindstone** is a stone used to sharpen tools. A **grinder** is a type of sandwich also called a submarine, hoagie, and hero.

Introduce Sight Words   Introduce the new sight word used in the lesson: *four.* Have students make up sentences using the word. Then ask the class to repeat the sight word and spell it aloud. Have them write the letters in the air using their fingers as a pencil. Add this word to the Word Wall or have students add it to their personal dictionaries.

Completing Student Pages 41–48

Identify any pictures that may be unfamiliar to students, such as *sight* in item 2 and *grill* in item 3 on page 41. Together, read the directions and then direct students to complete the pages independently, providing assistance as needed.

Fluency

Noting Punctuation   Ask volunteers to read sentences 4 and 6 on page 46, then read them aloud as a class. Remind students to pause when they see a comma. If students are having difficulty pausing at the correct place, have them continue practice reading the sentences with a partner until they pause correctly and read the sentences smoothly.

Repeated Reading   Have students read page 53 of "Day Care for Dogs!" from *Beyond The Code* Book 3. Model reading aloud while the class follows along. Then assign partners and have them take turns reading it to each other. Finally, ask students to read it in unison. Remind them to use appropriate expression when they encounter commas, semicolons, and exclamation points, and to emphasize boldface words, as necessary.

Comprehension

Extending Word Knowledge   Tell students that some words can have two or more different meanings. Give some examples: **cold** means "not hot" and "a common illness"; **roll** means "a small bun" and "to turn over and over." Read pairs of sentences and give both definitions. Have students put their thumbs up when they hear the correct meaning of the word. For example, say: *"I like to roll down the hill.* Does 'roll' mean 'a small bun' or 'to turn over and over'?" [thumbs up for the second definition] Other example words and definitions are **old**: "having lived a long time" and "not new"; **bolt**: "a small metal fastener" and "run away suddenly"; **mold**: "to form into a shape" and "a fungus."

Writing   Ask students to write clues for words using word families *-all, -alk, -old, -olt, -oll, -ild, -ind.* Students then trade papers with a partner to see if the partner can guess the words.

Differentiating Instruction

Extra Practice   For extra practice with the word families in this review lesson, have students complete the activities in *Explode The Code* Book 5½, Lesson 3.

Learning Styles (Visual)   Write five words from Lessons 3–5 on the board and ask students to copy the words in large letters on a piece of paper. Have students trace the letters of each word with markers, using a different color marker for the vowels. Then have students close their eyes and trace each word in the air in front of them, paying attention to the sequence of letters, their formation, and the sounds they make.

ELL   Ask a volunteer to choose one of the words from Lessons 3–5 and pantomime its meaning to the rest of the class. The student who guesses the word being pantomimed chooses a new word and takes the next turn.

Computer-based Reinforcement   Give students additional practice with word ending review on *ETC Online*, Units 5.6.2 to 5.6.7.

Lesson 7
qu words

Link to Prior Knowledge

Ask students what sound the letters *qu* make (/kw/). Say the words *queen, quiet, squish,* and *inquire,* and ask students to listen for the *kw* sound in each word. Tell students that this lesson is about /kw/ spelled *qu.*

Phonemic Awareness

Sound Isolation   Highlight the difference between /k/ and /kw/. Read the words below to the class, and have students tell you the sound they hear at the beginning of each word.

quiet (/kw/)	ketchup (/k/)
quit (/kw/)	kayak (/k/)
kite (/k/)	quack (/kw/)
quick (/kw/)	key (/k/)

Phonics

Introduce the Skill   Tell students that whenever they see the letter *q* in a word it will be followed by the vowel *u,* and that together they always make the sound /kw/. Tell students that they will be reading and writing words in this lesson that have the /kw/ sound spelled *qu.*

Write the following on the board: __ick, e__ip, ____it, s__eal, __een, s__eeze, __iz, __ack. Ask volunteers to fill in the blanks with the letters that say /kw/, then say the words aloud.

Vocabulary

Introduce New Vocabulary   If you are not sure whether students are familiar with certain lesson words or concepts, provide explanations. For example, before ballpoint pens were invented, people wrote with **quill** pens: long, stiff feathers dipped in ink. The pointy **quills** that stick out of the back of a porcupine are sharp. **Quicksand** is soft, wet sand that traps things. A **quail** is a type of small bird. Five people make up a **quintet**.

Introduce Sight Words   Introduce the new sight words used in the lesson: *says, some, water, out, someone, door, people,* and *won.* Have students make up sentences using each word. Then ask the class to repeat the sight words and spell them aloud. Have them write the letters in the air using their fingers as a pencil. Add these words to the Word Wall or have students add them to their personal dictionaries.

Completing Student Pages 49–56

Identify any pictures that may be unfamiliar to students, such as *squeeze* in item 5 and *fist* in item 6 on page 49. Together, read the directions and then direct students to complete the pages independently, providing assistance as needed.

Fluency

Have students read pages 40–41 of "Kal Grows Up and Up" from *Beyond The Code* Book 3. Model reading the first page aloud while the class follows along. Then assign partners and have them take turns reading it to each other. Finally, ask students to read it in unison. Remind them to use appropriate expression when they encounter commas, semicolons, and exclamation points, and to emphasize boldface words.

Phrasing   Tell students to think about word meanings as they read aloud. Suggest that they look for words that seem to belong together as a group of words, or phrase. Model reading one of the sentences on page 55, paying particular attention to phrasing. Then have students read the remaining sentences aloud several times.

Comprehension

Extending Word Knowledge   Ask students to answer the following questions, using /kw/ words from the lesson.

> You use this to cover up with and keep warm in the wintertime. (quilt)
> This is what you do with your eyes if you are trying to see something better. (squint)
> This is what you do to your thirst after taking a drink of water. (quench)
> Your teacher gives this small test when she or he wants to know what you've learned. (quiz)
> This is a group of five musicians. (quintet)
> If you repeat something someone else has said, you *blank* them. (quote)

Writing   Have students write five silly newspaper headlines that use at least two /kw/ words in each. Provide them with examples like *Queen Quacks Quietly* or *Quail Falls in Quicksand.*

Differentiating Instruction

Extra Practice   For extra practice with *qu,* have students complete the activities in *Explode The Code* Book 5½, Lesson 5.

ELL   Since the *qu* is pronounced /k/ and the *u* is silent in Spanish, Spanish speakers may have difficulty reading words such as *queen* and *quilt.* Make sure students have ample opportunities to practice saying these and other *qu* words, and using them in context.

Challenge   Students who complete these pages without difficulty can play a rhyme game. Write ten words from this lesson on the board. Ask students to read the words silently, then think of rhyming words to write down. Give students two minutes; adjust time if necessary. Whoever has written down the most real words wins the game.

Computer-based Reinforcement   Give students additional practice with *qu* words on *ETC Online,* Units 5.7.2 to 5.7.7.

Lesson 8
thr, shr, and *scr* words

Link to Prior Knowledge

In Book 2, students learned that words can begin with two consonants whose sounds are blended together when spoken. Say the words *flag, crab, black,* and *green,* emphasizing the blends at the beginning of the words. Students also learned that the digraph *th* makes the sound /th/ and the digraph *sh* makes the sound /sh/. Explain to students that rules for blends and digraphs still apply when three consonants appear together, and that is what this lesson is about.

Phonemic Awareness

Word Rhyming   Tell students you are going to say groups of three words and you want them to listen to how the words end. After each set of words, ask them which two words sound alike at the end.

chip, throne, shone (throne, shone)   thrill, treat, spill (thrill, spill)
scratch, hatch, skit (scratch, hatch)   ring, shrink, stink (shrink, stink)
scream, steam, step (scream, steam)   shred, bread, chat (shred, bread)

Phonics

Introduce the Skill   Tell students that in this lesson they will be reading and writing words that begin with the *thr, scr,* and *shr* blends.

Make a three-column chart labeled "blends," "rimes," and "words" on the board and ask each student to make one. In the left column write *thr, scr, shr,* and in the right column write *ee, imp, atch, ink, ug, row, ill, eam, ub, een, oat, amble, ap, ape.* Ask students to combine the blends in the first column with the rimes in the second column to make *thr, scr,* and *shr* words, and write them in the third column labeled "words."

Vocabulary

Introduce New Vocabulary   If you are not sure whether students are familiar with certain lesson words or concepts, provide explanations. For example, a **shrub** is a small bush. To **shrug** is to raise and lower your shoulders. To **shred** is to rip up. A **script** is the text of a play.

Introduce Sight Words   Introduce the new sight words used in the lesson: *any, anything, watch, should,* and *do.* Have students make up sentences using each word. Then ask the class to repeat the sight words and spell them aloud. Have them write the letters in the air using their fingers as a pencil. Add these words to the Word Wall or have students add them to their personal dictionaries.

Completing Student Pages 57–64

Identify any pictures that may be unfamiliar to students, such as *stretch* in item 4 on page 57. Together, read the directions and then direct students to complete the pages independently, providing assistance as needed.

Fluency

Articulation   Assign partners and have students practice reading the sentences on page 63, enunciating all the sounds they hear in the words. Then switch so the other partner can practice reading.

Comprehension

Extending Word Knowledge   Remind students that some words can have two or more different meanings. Give some examples: **scrambled** means "mixed together" and "ran fast"; **screen** means "a surface to watch television or movies" and "a frame of fine wire over a window to keep insects out." Read pairs of sentences and give both definitions. Have students put their thumbs up when they hear the correct meaning of the word. For example, say: *"The goat scrambled down the mountain.* Does 'scrambled' mean 'ran fast' [thumbs up] or 'mixed together'?" Another example word and definition is **scratch**: "a mark made by something sharp" and "to rub an itch."

Writing   Have students make up silly names for foods, using several *thr, shr,* and *scr* words. Provide some examples like *three-decker shrimp sandwich* or *scrambled and shredded eggs.*

Differentiating Instruction

Extra Practice   For extra practice with *thr, shr,* and *scr* words, have students complete the activities in *Explode The Code* Book 5½, Lesson 6.

Learning Styles (Visual)   Ask students to choose one of the three blends studied in this lesson. In the middle of a piece of paper, have them write the blend and draw a circle around it. Then have them draw pictures of words beginning with their chosen blend.

Challenge   Have students who complete these pages without difficulty create a do-it-yourself crossword puzzle, using *thr, shr,* and *scr* words. Show students an example of a crossword puzzle grid. Direct students to make a list of words to use, and help them each make a blank crossword grid to fit the words. They should then write clues for the words. Have them switch puzzles with a friend and try to complete it.

Computer-based Reinforcement   Give students additional practice with *thr, shr,* and *scr* words on *ETC Online,* Units 5.8.2 to 5.8.6.

Lesson 9
str, spr, and *spl* words

Quick Review

In the previous lesson, students learned that words can begin with three consonants whose individual sounds are blended together to make one sound. Ask students to name some of these words, and write the words on the board.

Say the words *strong, spray,* and *split.* Tell students that this lesson is about the three-letter consonant blends *str, spr,* and *spl.*

Phonemic Awareness

Phoneme Blending   Say the words below and have students listen for the consonant blends at the beginning of the words. Tell students to *scratch* (emphasize the *scr* in *scratch*) the tops of their heads when they hear a word with a three-consonant blend.

scrabble (scratch)	split (scratch)
scared	spit
stick	script (scratch)
strict (scratch)	skipped
slit	sprint (scratch)

Phonics

Introduce the Skill   Tell students that in this lesson they will be reading and writing words that begin with *str* as in *strong, spr* as in *spray,* and *spl* as in *split.*

Write the following words on the board: *splinter, sprint, strong, street, splash, splendid.* Ask volunteers to draw a circle around the letters that make up the consonant blend in each word. Then have them say the words and write them.

Vocabulary

Introduce New Vocabulary   If you are not sure whether students are familiar with certain lesson words or concepts, provide explanations. For example, if you're running at top speed for just a short distance, you're **sprinting**. A **streamlined** car is shaped to make it faster. To **split** is to divide. To **spring** means to jump, and **spring** is also a season. To **struggle** is to try hard to do something.

Introduce Sight Words Introduce the new sight word used in the lesson: *American*. Have students make up sentences using the word. Then ask the class to repeat the sight word and spell it aloud. Have them write the letters in the air using their fingers as a pencil. Add this word to the Word Wall or have students add it to their personal dictionaries.

Completing Student Pages 65–72

Identify any pictures that may be unfamiliar to students, such as *stream* in item 3 or *spin* in item 4 on page 65. Together, read the directions and then direct students to complete the pages independently, providing assistance as needed.

Fluency

Repeated Reading Have students read page 88 of "Kate and Her Ten-Speed Bike" from *Beyond The Code* Book 3. Model reading aloud while the class follows along. Then assign partners and have them take turns reading it to each other. Finally, ask students to read it in unison. Remind them to use appropriate expression when they encounter commas, semi-colons, and exclamation points, and to emphasize boldface words, as necessary.

Comprehension

Extending Word Knowledge Remind students that some words can have two or more different meanings. Give some examples: **key** means "a small metal object that closes a lock" and "something that is very important"; **squash** means "a type of vegetable that grows on a vine" and "to press flat." Read pairs of sentences and give both definitions. Have students put their thumbs up when they hear the correct meaning of the word. For example, say: "*The teacher read the list of key words to the class.* Does 'key' mean 'a small metal object that closes a lock' or 'something that is very important'?" [thumbs up]

Writing Provide students with the following story starters and ask them to write a short story. Encourage students to use as many *str, spr,* and *spl* words as they can.

> The cat **sprang** from the tree . . .
> The frog made a big **splash** in the **stream** . . .

Differentiating Instruction

Extra Practice For extra practice with *str, spr,* and *spl* words, have students complete the activities in *Explode The Code* Book 5½, Lesson 7.

ELL Because some Asian languages, in particular, do not differentiate between *s* and *sh*, students may have difficulty with blends that begin with *s*. Have students practice saying the sounds separately a few times, then blend them together: /s/ /t/ /r/ /ing/, *string;* /s/ /p/ /r/ /out/, *sprout;* /s/ /p/ /l/ /it/, *split.*

Challenge   Have students who complete these pages without difficulty write questions that can be answered with one of the *str, spr,* or *spl* words from this lesson. After writing the questions, have them trade with a friend and see if they can answer each other's questions. Examples: I can't wait for winter to be over and *blank* to start (spring). Tie the *blank* in a loop (string).

Computer-based Reinforcement   Give students additional practice with *str, spr,* and *spl* words on *ETC Online*, Units 5.9.2 to 5.9.6.

Lesson 10
-*ey* words

Link to Prior Knowledge
Ask students what sound the letter *e* makes in words like *Pete, steam,* and *feed* (/ē/). Ask students for additional examples of silent *e, ee,* and *ea* words that have the long *e* sound. Ask students if they remember what *y* says at the end of two-syllable words (/ē/). Have students think of some two-syllable words that end in *y* and write them on the board. Tell students that -*ey* is another way of spelling the long *e* sound at the end of words.

Phonemic Awareness
Sound Matching   Say the following words and have students clap when they hear a word that ends with the long *e* sound.

stronger	sprinting
monkey (clap)	valley (clap)
money (clap)	leaving
snuggle	chimney (clap)
hockey (clap)	

Phonics
Introduce the Skill   Tell students that many words that end in -*ey* say /ē/ at the end. In this lesson they will be reading and writing some of these words.

Tell students to say the sound /ē/, then the word *key*. Pass out index cards and have students write -*ey* on the front and draw a picture of a key on the back. Ask if they can think of any other words that end with -*ey* (*monkey, donkey, hockey, money, honey*). Write them on the board and have students copy them on the side of the index card with the key.

Vocabulary

Introduce New Vocabulary If you are not sure whether students are familiar with certain lesson words or concepts, provide explanations. For example, a **valley** is a low space between two hills. A **trolley** is a type of train that runs on tracks on the street. The **jockey** is the person who rides the horse in a horse race. A **pulley** is a tool that makes things easier to lift.

Introduce Sight Words Introduce the new sight word used in the lesson: *tossed.* Have students make up sentences using the word. Then ask the class to repeat the sight word and spell it. Have them write the letters in the air using their fingers as a pencil. Add this word to the Word Wall or have students add it to their personal dictionaries.

Completing Student Pages 73–80

Identify any pictures that may be unfamiliar to students, such as *pointed* in item 4, *pulley* in item 3, and *pole vault* in item 5 on page 73; and *jockey* in row 1 on page 74. Together, read the directions and then direct students to complete the pages independently, providing assistance as needed.

Fluency

Read with Expression Remind students to read with expression by changing the volume (loudness) and pitch (high and low sounds) of their voice as they read aloud. Read the sentences on page 76 with exaggerated expression to model expressive reading. Then have students whisper-read it themselves.

Comprehension

Ask students the following questions and have them answer using -ey words from the lesson.

> You can get milk from a cow. What does a bee make? (honey)
> You can keep a hammer in a toolbox. What do you keep in your wallet? (money)
> In soccer you play with a ball. In which sport do you play with a puck? (hockey)
> Something that sticks up from the top of a car is an antenna. What sticks up from the top of a house? (chimney)
> A racecar driver rides in a car. Who rides on a racehorse? (jockey)
> Mountains reach up into the sky. What is between mountains, that dips down to the ground? (valley)
> A person lives in a house. What animal lives in the zoo? (monkey)

Writing Provide students with the following story starters and ask them to write a short story. Encourage students to use as many -ey words as they can.

> A **donkey** blocked the **trolley** track . . .
> The **hockey** player could not find his **keys** . . .

Differentiating Instruction

Learning Styles (Visual)   Write five words from this lesson on the board and ask students to copy the words in large letters on a piece of paper. Have students trace the letters of each word with markers, using a different color for the vowels. Then have students close their eyes and trace each word in the air in front of them, paying attention to the sequence of letters, their formation, and the sounds they make.

ELL   In Spanish and some Asian languages the long *e* sound is written as *i,* so students who speak these languages may have difficulty with the long *e* sound spelled *ey.* To review, write *-ey* words on the board and have students practice saying them, circling the letters that make the long *e* sound. Then practice spelling the words aloud and repeat them.

Computer-based Reinforcement   Give students additional practice with *-ey* words on *ETC Online,* Units 5.10.2 to 5.10.7.

Lesson 11
Review Lesson

Cumulative Review

Toss a ball to a student as you say a word from Lessons 1–10. Have the student spell the word and toss the ball back to you. Continue until all students have had a turn.

Phonemic Awareness

Discriminating Sounds   Have students listen as you say several sets of words. Ask volunteers to tell you which words rhyme.

mild, wind, wild (mild, wild)	told, stroll, troll (stroll, troll)
sky, monkey, donkey (monkey, donkey)	chalk, chair, talk (chalk, talk)
fall, walk, wall (fall, wall)	bend, bind, find (bind, find)
fainted, painted, dashed (fainted, painted)	colt, cold, bold (cold, bold)

Phonics

Skill Review   For each set of words below, say the first word and ask a volunteer to write it on the board. Ask a second volunteer to add a letter or letters to the first word to build a new word.

ash, lash, splash, splashed	ray, tray, stray, straying
old, cold, scold, scolded	all, mall, small, smaller
ring, string, stringing	

Vocabulary

Introduce New Vocabulary　If you are not sure whether students are familiar with certain lesson words or concepts, provide explanations. For example, a **splinter** is a little piece of wood stuck under your skin. If you **blended** some batter, you mixed it until it is smooth. If you **constructed** something, it means you built it.

Introduce Sight Words　Introduce the new sight word used in the lesson: *also*. Have students make up sentences using the word. Then ask the class to repeat the sight word and spell it. Have them write the letters in the air using their fingers as a pencil. Add this word to the Word Wall or have students add it to their personal dictionaries.

Completing Student Pages 81–88

Identify any pictures that may be unfamiliar to students, such as *crust* in item 5 on page 81. Together, read the directions and then direct students to complete the pages independently, providing assistance as needed.

Fluency

Word Automaticity　Students should be able to say the words from each lesson easily and clearly, and apply skills they've learned to new words. Have students practice reading sentences from pages 84 and 87, thinking about the meaning of the words as they read and using proper emphasis, pitch, and volume. Then ask students to take turns reading a sentence aloud to the rest of the class.

Repeated Reading　Have students read page 21 of "What's the Fuss?" from *Beyond The Code* Book 3. Model reading aloud while the class follows along. Then assign partners and have them take turns reading it to each other. Finally, ask students to read it in unison. Remind them to use appropriate expression when they encounter commas, semicolons, and exclamation points, and to emphasize boldface words, as necessary.

Comprehension

Write a word from each of the previous lessons on an index card. Hold up the cards one by one and ask volunteers to say the word and use it in a sentence.

Writing　Ask students to write a story using at least two skill words from each lesson.

Differentiating Instruction
Extra Practice　For extra practice with the skills in Book 5, have students complete the activities in *Explode The Code* Book 5½, Lesson 11.

Computer-based Reinforcement　Give students additional practice on *ETC Online*, Units 5.11.2 to 5.11.7.

Book 5 Posttest Pages 89–92

You may wish to have students complete the pages of the posttest in more than one sitting. Read each set of directions with students. Observe as students begin working independently to be sure they understand how to complete each page. Introduce the sight word *their*.

Page 89. Give the instruction "Circle the word you hear," and dictate the words listed below. students circle the correct word from a choice of five words.

> 1. childlike; 2. sidewalk; 3. connected; 4. streamlined; 5. billfold; 6. shrunken; 7. hallway; 8. conducted; 9. behind; 10. inspected

Page 90. Students write sentences dictated by the teacher. Dictate each sentence slowly once or twice. It is often helpful for students to repeat the sentence before they write it.

> 1. The dog has cold meatballs in its dish.
> 2. The child played baseball with his pals.
> 3. The queen holds a gold key in her hand.
> 4. Patty hunted for the wild tiger cat.
> 5. Will you find three mistakes on this paper?

Pages 91–92. Students complete these pages on their own. Simple directions are included at the top of each worksheet.

Page 91. Students write the words that best complete the sentences.

> 1. cold; 2. ball; 3. quack; 4. throne; 5. key; 6. splash

Page 92. Students read short paragraphs and select words from a list to complete each paragraph sensibly.

> 1. child, behind, bolt, key, springs
> 2. splendid, roller coaster, hold, screamed, cold cuts, money
> 3. clapped, struck, crashed, tallest, thrilled

Book 5½ Posttest Pages 89–92

Page 89. Give the instruction "Circle the word you hear," and dictate the words listed below. The students circle the correct word from a choice of five words.

> 1. mildness; 2. goldfinch; 3. expected; 4. kindliness; 5. zippered; 6. scaffolding; 7. chalkboard; 8. postponed; 9. screeching; 10. callback

Page 90. Students write sentences dictated by the teacher. Dictate each sentence slowly once or twice. It is often helpful for students to repeat the sentence before they write it.

> 1. It was a splendid day to roller skate.
> 2. Clem throws the scrapbook in the rusted trashcan.
> 3. Kim fished for squid in the frozen stream.
> 4. The queen dumped a quart of milk on the throne.

5. Mom scolded Liz for screaming and being wild.
6. Zack quickly opened the bag of salted pretzels.

Pages 91–92. Students complete these pages on their own. Simple directions are included at the top of each worksheet.

Page 91. Students write the words that best complete the sentences.

    1. stained; 2. screamed; 3. quarter; 4. scratching; 5. wildest; 6. unrolled

Page 92. Students read short paragraphs and select words from a list to complete each paragraph sensibly.

    1. Goldilocks, folks, coldness, unfolded, behold, scolded, told
    2. snowfall, tallest, halted, walrus, rolled, behind, wallet, fallen, wild

Posttest Scores

- **80% of items correct (60 out of 75 total):** Mastery of skills presented in Book 5.
- **Less than 80% of items correct:** Review skills in Book 5 as needed.

Book 6

Lesson 1
ar words

Link to Prior Knowledge

Ask students to name some examples of short *a* words (*nap, plan, last*). Then have them name words starting with *r* (*rope, rest, real*). Ask students to say the sound for the letter *r* /r/, then the name of the letter (är). Explain that combining short *a* with *r* can say /är/, which sounds like the name for the letter *r*. Tell students that this lesson is about words containing /är/.

Phonemic Awareness

Discriminating Sounds   Ask students to listen as you say several words. Have them show thumbs up or thumbs down to indicate whether they hear /är/ in each word.

stand (thumbs down)	dark (thumbs up)
start (thumbs up)	rake (thumbs down)
arm (thumbs up)	garden (thumbs up)
bran (thumbs down)	backyard (thumbs up)
barn (thumbs up)	

Phonics

Introduce the Skill   Explain to students that many words contain /är/ spelled *a-r*, and they will be reading and writing some of them in this lesson.

Draw a five-pointed star on the board and have students identify it. Write the word *star* underneath, and say it. Explain that when *ar* is in a word, it changes the vowel sound. Have students say the word *star* again. Circle the *ar* and pronounce the word slowly, emphasizing the *är* sound.

Now say the word *cat*. Have students tell you how to spell it, and write it on the board. Say the word *cart* and demonstrate how to spell it. Contrast the two vowel sounds of short *a* and *är*. Work with the sets *pat/part* and *had/hard,* having students dictate the spellings for both words in the set.

Vocabulary

Introduce New Vocabulary   If you are not sure that students are familiar with certain lesson words or concepts, provide explanations. For example, **varnish** is a shiny coating painted on furniture. A **dart** is a short, sharp arrow. If you **dart** from place to place, you run quickly. A **target** is something you aim at, like in a game of darts. A **spark** is a tiny flash of light from a fire. When an animal **snarls**, it growls and shows its teeth.

Introduce Sight Words   Introduce the new sight words used in the lesson: *many, would, have,* and *your.* Have students make up sentences using the words. Then ask the class to repeat the sight words and spell them aloud. Have them write the letters in the air using their fingers as a pencil. Add these words to the Word Wall or have students add them to their personal dictionaries.

Introduce Direction Words   The words *sentence, write, circle,* and *police* are used in the directions for this book. If you want students to learn to read these words, introduce them in the way you introduce the sight words.

Completing Student Pages 1–8

Identify any pictures that may be unfamiliar to students, such as *cold* in item 3, *build* in item 6, and *party* and *park* in item 7 on page 1; and *harp* in row 3 on page 2. Together, read the directions and work through a sample item on each page. Then direct students to complete the pages independently, providing assistance as needed.

Fluency

Improving Accuracy   Have partners pick two or three pairs of sentences from page 7 and practice reading them to each other smoothly and accurately.

Comprehension

Synonyms and Antonyms   Write the following /är/ words on the board: *market, sparkle, dark, smart, jar, darted, carpet, hard.* Have students choose from these words to fill in the blanks in the sentences below. Read the sentences aloud and provide visual clues, if possible; some suggestions are provided.

1. Which word means the opposite of *soft*? (stroke your hand) **hard** (clap your hands once, or knock on a desk or the board)
2. Which word means the opposite of *unintelligent*? **smart**
3. Which word means the opposite of *bright*? (shade your eyes) **dark** (cover your eyes, or turn out the lights)
4. Which word means the opposite of *strolled*? (walk slowly) **darted** (move quickly toward the door)
5. Which word means *shimmer* or *twinkle*? **sparkle**
6. Which word means *grocery store*? **market**
7. Which word means *container*? **jar**
8. Which word means *rug*? **carpet**

Writing   Ask students to complete the story starter below. Direct them to write at least three sentences, including two or three more /är/ words.

When I looked in the mirror this morning I was **startled** to see . . .

Differentiating Instruction
Extra Practice   For extra practice reading and writing /är/ words, have students complete the activities in *Explode The Code* Book 6½, Lesson 1.

Learning Styles (Visual)   Have visual learners draw a big five-pointed star and write *star* in the middle. Then have them choose five other /är/ words to write in each arm of the star.

ELL   Many Asian alphabets, including Vietnamese, Hmong, and Korean, do not include the *är* sound, so native speakers may have difficulty with this and other vowel plus *r* sounds. Be sure to emphasize the *r* sound in target words, especially when contrasting short *a* and *är*, such as *match* and *march* on page 2.

Challenge   Students who complete these pages without difficulty can do a word-within-a-word search. Have them list all the /är/ words in the lesson that contain the word *car* (*scar, scarf, card, cart, carpet*) and *art* (*party, dart, darted, cart, artist*). Assign other /är/ words to search for (*arm, ark*, etc).

Computer-based Reinforcement   Give students additional practice with *ar* words on *ETC Online*, Units 6.1.2 to 6.1.7.

Lesson 2
or words

Quick Review
Have students each draw a picture of a star on notecards. Have them hold up their cards with the star side facing them. They should turn the star side front only when they hear you say a word that contains /är/. Slowly say these words: *pay, pat, part, frame, farm, fan, carve, chart, snack, shark.* Tell students that next they will learn how *r* changes the sound of the letter *o*.

Phonemic Awareness
Discriminating Sounds   Tell students that now they should listen for a different vowel plus *r* sound—/ôr/. Say some sample words (*more, horse, short*). Then say some more words and have students show thumbs up if the words contain /ôr/ and thumbs down if they do not: *farm, for, pot, fork, stop, storm, score, scar.*

Phonics

Introduce the Skill   Explain that in this lesson, students will learn to read and spell another vowel plus *r* combination that appears in many words: *o-r* pronounced the same as the word *or*. Write *or* in the upper corner of the board. Have students write the letters *or* on one side of a card and draw a picture of a *fork* on the back. Write *fork* on the board and ask students to name rhyming words (*cork, pork, stork*). Write the words below *fork*.

Then write the letters *c* and *n* on the board with two blanks in the middle (c__ __n). Ask students what vegetable can be eaten "on the cob." Then ask a volunteer to finish spelling the word *corn* as you say it. Elicit and list other words that rhyme with *corn* (*born, horn, thorn, torn, worn*). Have volunteers circle the /ôr/ spellings.

Vocabulary

Introduce New Vocabulary   If you are not sure that students are familiar with certain lesson words or concepts, provide explanations. For example, people hold **torches** to see in the dark. **Shortcake** is a kind of cake. A **fort** or **fortress** is a big protected place. An **organ** is a musical instrument. An **orchard** is a group of fruit trees. A **thorn** is a sharp point on a plant stem. A **stork** is a type of bird. A **harbor** is place where ships anchor.

Introduce Sight Words   Introduce the new sight words used in the lesson: *there, does,* and *was.* Have students make up sentences using each word. Then ask the class to repeat the sight words and spell them aloud. Have them write the letters in the air using their fingers as a pencil. Add these words to the Word Wall or have students add them to their personal dictionaries.

Completing Student Pages 9–16

Identify pictures that may be unfamiliar to students, such as *thorn* in item 3, *torch* in item 5, and *cord* in item 6 on page 11. Together, read the directions and work through a sample item on each page. Then direct students to complete the pages independently, providing assistance as needed.

Fluency

Developing Accuracy   Write the following tongue twisters on sentence strips and have students practice reading them aloud to a partner:

> Fran finds **forty** farms and fifty **forts**.
> Ann ate crab, **corn**, clams, and crackers.
> The **short** silly **stork** is shy.

Comprehension

Antonyms   Have students think of an *or* word that is opposite in meaning to the words you present. Write the words on the board. Give an example: The opposite of tall is . . . (short).

less (more)   remembered (forgot)
night (morning)   exciting (boring)
south (north)   backward (forward)
sunny (stormy)

Writing   Have students write their own tongue twisters, including at least two /ôr/ words from the lesson. Have volunteers read their tongue twisters aloud.

Differentiating Instruction
Extra Practice   For extra practice reading and writing /ôr/ words, have students complete the activities in *Explode The Code* Book 6½, Lesson 2.

Learning Styles (Auditory)   Give auditory learners additional experience with /ôr/ by asking them to listen and tell you what word you are spelling. Tell them you will repeat each word twice and pause between the syllables in multisyllabic words. Slowly spell: *storm, porch, hor/net, cor/ner, for/tress, or/der/ling.*

Challenge   Students who complete these pages without difficulty can be given the following lists of words: *short, north, horse, storm, corn, stork, snore.* Challenge them to write a short story including all seven words at least once, and have them share their stories with the class.

Computer-based Reinforcement   Give students additional practice with *or* words on *ETC Online,* Units 6.2.2 to 6.2.7.

Lesson 3
er, ir, ur **words**

Quick Review
Give students two index cards and have them write *ar* on one and *or* on the other. Tell them you are going to say some words and you want them to raise the card that represents the vowel sound in the word: *target, border, starring, stork, horrid, torpedo, carpenter.*

Phonemic Awareness
Sound Substitution   Model how to substitute initial consonant sounds to make new words: "The word is *torn.* [Emphasize initial consonant sound.] If I change /t/ to /th/, I get *thorn."* Have students do the following:

1. The word is *fork.* Change /f/ to /p/. What do you get? (pork)
2. The word is *sport.* Change /sp/ to /sh/. What do you get? (short)
3. The word is *floor.* Change /fl/ to /st/. What do you get? (store)
4. The word is *chore.* Change /ch/ to /sh/. What do you get? (shore)
5. The word is *torch.* Change /t/ to /p/. What do you get? (porch)
6. The word is *pouring.* Change /p/ to /b/. What do you get? (boring)

Phonics

Introduce the Skill　Tell students that they will be working with words that contain the *er* sound. Explain that they will learn three different ways to spell /er/. Draw a girl's face, point to it, and say, "I am pointing to *her.*" Label the picture *her,* underlining the /er/ spelling. Follow the same procedure for *bird* (draw a bird, point to a bird in the sky, or flap your arms; say, "Can you see a *bird* in the sky?") and *burn* (draw a picture of a campfire on the board; say, "The fire will *burn* until we put it out.") Elicit what is the same about these words (they all rhyme and have same *er* sound) and different about them (different spellings for /er/).

　　Say a list of words and have students put their thumbs up when they hear a word with /er/ (this can be spelled either *er, ir,* or *ur*): *bird, hot, hurt, scare shirt, perch, part, burn, forty, fern.* Write the words with the *er* sounds on the board as students identify them, circling the letters that say /er/.

Vocabulary

Introduce New Vocabulary　If students are not familiar with lesson words or concepts, provide explanations: When you **jerk** something, you pull it quickly. To **disturb** means to bother. A **fern** is a type of leafy plant. You **furnish** a room when you put furniture in it. A snake is a **serpent**. A **nursery** is a room for a baby. A **carport** is a shelter for a car that has open sides. A **perch** is where a bird rests.

Introduce Sight Words　Introduce the new sight word used in the lesson: *water.* Have students make up sentences using the word. Then ask the class to repeat the sight word and spell it aloud. Have them write the letters in the air using their fingers as a pencil. Add the word to the Word Wall or have students add it to their personal dictionaries.

Completing Student Pages 17–24

Identify any pictures that may be unfamiliar to students, such as *serve* in item 3 and *dirt* in item 4 of page 17, in addition to the swimmer who has come in *first* in row 1 on page 18. When they are ready, have students complete the pages independently, providing assistance as needed.

Fluency

Noting Punctuation　Remind students that when they read a sentence that ends with a question mark, their voices should rise at the end. Model reading the first three questions on page 20, then have students practice reading them aloud. Listen to see if they are using proper intonation for a question.

Comprehension

If necessary, explain that a "hink pink" is a silly riddle with an answer made up of two rhyming words. Write this example on the board and read it to students: *What do you call a spiral hairdo on a young lady? (girl's curls)* Have students note that the answer is two /er/ words that rhyme, and discuss the answer to make sure students understand why it fits the riddle. Then have students solve the following hink pinks. If they have any trouble, provide the first word of the answer.

1. What do you do if you mix dog hair into cake batter? (stir fur)
2. What do you get from touching a sizzling-hot leafy plant? (fern burn)
3. What do you call an injured piece of girls' clothing? (hurt skirt)
4. What do you call the handbags carried by people who work with doctors? (nurses' purses)
5. In a row of three feathered animals, this is the last one. (third bird)

Writing   Have students select one of the pictures on page 23 to write a short story about, including at least four /er/ words. Remind them that their story should tell who, where, when, and what happened.

Differentiating Instruction

Extra Practice   Pass out seven letter tiles or cards to each student: *e, h, i, r, s, t,* and *u.* Then provide practice spelling various /er/ words (for example: *her, sir, stir, hurt, shirt, hurts, thirst*) using the following procedure. Use the word in a short oral sentence, then repeat the target word. Have students assemble the word using their tiles. Depending on the degree of support, you may want to put the first letter(s) on the board and then have students use their tile spellings to tell you how to spell the rest of the word.

Learning Styles (Kinesthetic)   Put various /er/ words on the board, being sure to cover all three spellings (*er, ir,* and *ur*). Have students say each word with you, then air spell it with their fingers. Point to each word and ask: "How do you spell /er/ in this word?" Have students respond by saying and air-spelling the correct /er/ spelling.

Challenge   For students who complete these pages without difficulty, write the following word pairs on the board: *fur/fir, turn/tern, birth/berth.* Explain that the words in each pair are homophones: words that sound alike but are spelled differently. Students may choose just one homophone pair to work with, or they may work with all three. Have them provide word meaning (using a dictionary as needed) for each word in the pair, then create sentences using both words. They may illustrate the sentences, if they wish.

Computer-based Reinforcement   Give students additional practice with *er, ir,* and *ur* words on *ETC Online,* Units 6.3.2 to 6.3.7.

Lesson 4
wor and *war* words

Link to Prior Knowledge

Have students name and spell one or two words that contain the /ôr/ sound. Then have them name some /är/ and /er/ words and spell them.

Phonemic Awareness

Sound Substitution   Model how to substitute initial consonant sounds to make new words: "The word is *firm.* [Emphasize initial consonant sound.] If I change /f/ to /w/, I get *worm.*" Have students do the following:

1. The word is *jerk.* Change /j/ to /w/. What do you get? (work)
2. The word is *bird.* Change /b/ to /w/. What do you get? (word)
3. The word is *tore.* Change /t/ to /w/. What do you get? (war)
4. The word is *fort.* Change /f/ to /w/. What do you get? (wart)
5. The word is *morning.* Change /m/ to /w/. What do you get? (warning)
6. The word is *thirst.* Change /th/ to /w/. What do you get? (worst)

Phonics

Introducing the Skill   List the first few words you worked with in Phonemic Awareness in a chart, putting *firm, jerk, bird,* and *thirst* in one column and *worm, work, word,* and *worst* in the other. Have students come up to say each word and underline its /er/ spelling. Then extend their underlining in the second column to include the *w*. Point out that when *w* combines with *or,* it makes the sound *wer.* Follow a similar procedure with *tore, fort, morning,* and the *war-* words, where *w* plus *ar* makes the sound *wôr.*

Vocabulary

Introduce New Vocabulary   If students are unfamiliar with lesson words or concepts, provide explanations: **Morn** means the same as **morning**. To **warble** is to sing like a bird. If something is **worthwhile**, it has value. Your **wardrobe** includes all your clothes. A **swarm** of bees is a large group of bees.

Introduce Sight Words   Introduce the new sight words used in the lesson: *their, were, place, our, about, could,* and *watch.* Have students make up sentences using the words. Then ask the class to repeat the sight words and spell them aloud. Have them write the letters in the air using their fingers as a pencil. Add these words to the Word Wall or have students add them to their personal dictionaries.

Completing Student Pages 25–32

Identify any pictures that may be unfamiliar to students, such as *war* in item 4 and *wart* in item 5 on page 25; the *backward* letter *r* in row 4 on page 29; and the three people at a pond in winter on page 31. Then direct students to complete the pages on their own, providing assistance as necessary.

Fluency

Improving Rate   Have students choral read their completed sentences on page 30. Guide them to set a pace that moves along smoothly but still allows them time to pronounce the words clearly and accurately. Then reread students' favorite sentences as a group, at a slightly faster pace.

Comprehension

Extending Word Knowledge   Have students discuss the answers to the following questions to demonstrate their understanding of lesson words.

1. What kind of thing would make you *worry*?
2. Who can tell me two words that describe a *worm*?
3. What kind of *work* do you do at home?
4. What can you do to get *warm*?
5. What would you *warn* someone about?

Writing   Ask students to draw a picture of the *world* and write five sentences about it. Each sentence has to include a *war* or *wor* word (other than *world*).

Differentiating Instruction

Learning Styles (Visual)   Have visual learners write a red *w* on a notecard. Write the following words in the middle of the board, where students can easily read them: *far, harm, cord,* and *cork.* For each word, have students take turns coming to the board, reading the word, covering the first letter with their *w* card, and saying the new word.

ELL   Some students may have trouble with *war* and *wor* words because many Asian languages, in particular, don't contain vowel plus *r* combinations or because their language does not contain a *w* sound (for example, Korean, Vietnamese, Russian, and German). Provide extra practice with *wor* and *war* by working with students to complete pages 25–32 of *Explode The Code* Book 6½.

Challenge   Students who complete these pages without difficulty can create three-line word chains. Using the words below as examples, have students write clues describing each word. Show students that each word in the chain grows by adding one letter to the beginning or end of the word before it. Have them come up with their own clues and new word chains. For the examples below: 1. (a) battle (b) area of a hospital (c) something you win; 2. (a) body part attached to your shoulder (b) not cold (c) a large group.

1. war, ward, award
2. arm, warm, swarm

Computer-based Reinforcement   Give students additional practice with *wor* and *war* words on *ETC Online*, Units 6.4.2 to 6.4.7.

Lesson 5
Review Lesson

Cumulative Review

Remind students that in the previous four lessons they learned about words containing different vowel plus *r* sounds and spellings. Write these headings on the board: *ar, or, er, ir, ur, wor, war*. As you point to each heading, say the associated sound and ask students to name a few words that contain this sound. Don't list any words yet, but keep the headings on the board.

Phonemic Awareness

Matching Sounds   Tell students to listen as you say groups of three words. Then have them identify the word whose vowel sound is different from the other two. As you say each word in the set, emphasize the vowel sound. For example: *sing, bark, harm* (sing)

harm, charm, bird (bird)	perch, torn, wore (perch)
worm, hope, term (hope)	serve, bark, term (bark)
stand, band, start (start)	park, fort, part (fort)

Vocabulary

Introduce New Vocabulary   If students are unfamiliar with certain review words or concepts, provide explanations: You can carry a **lantern** to see in the dark. To **forbid** means to order someone not to do something. A **mummy** is a monster all wrapped up in bandages. To **spar** means to pretend–fight. **Whirlwind** can be another name for a tornado. A **platform** is a raised surface, like a stage.

Introduce Sight Words   Introduce the new sight word used in the lesson: *around*. Have students make up sentences using the word. Then ask the class to repeat the sight word and spell it aloud. Have them write the letters in the air using their fingers as a pencil. Add this word to the Word Wall or have students add it to their personal dictionaries.

Completing Student Pages 33–40

Identify any pictures that may be unfamiliar to students, such as the *corner* of the two house walls in item 3, the *birchbark* covering the tree in item 5, and the gum bubble about to *burst* in item 7 on page 33; the *carport* in item 1 on page 35; and the lines that stand for *darkness* in item 4 on page 39. When students are ready, direct them to complete the pages on their own.

Fluency

Read with Expression   Direct students to look at page 20 and the top of page 21 of "What a Scare!" from *Beyond The Code* Book 4 while you read the passages aloud to them. Then assign partners and have them read the passages to each other. Tell them to think about the meaning of the words and the sentences as they read aloud, using their voices to show feelings. How does your voice sound if you are scared?

Comprehension

Have students think of a vowel plus *r* word that is opposite in meaning to the words you present. Write the words on the board. Give an example: "The opposite of long is . . ." (short).

small (large)   daylight (darkness)
cool (warm)   easy (hard)
last (first)   straightaway (turn)

Writing   Have students choose three of the following vowel plus *r* characters to include in a story: a *charming* monster, a shy *turtle,* a *swarm* of bees, a *thirsty bird*, a brave *worm,* and a sad *stork.* They can use their workbook pages from Lessons 1–4 as a source for other vowel plus *r* words to include in their story. Tell students to make sure the story has a beginning, middle, and end.

Differentiating Instruction

Learning Styles (Visual)   Have visual learners design and decorate a giant lowercase *r* in the center of a sheet of paper. Around the *r* have them write various vowel plus *r* words, written in different colors by category, from Lessons 1-4.

Extra Practice   Have students work together to make word cards of vowel plus *r* words. They can quiz each other for spelling, then read the words together and make up sentences for each one.

Challenge   Invite students to turn their stories from the Writing exercise into comic book adventures with pictures, or to write a second adventure for the same characters. Ask them to underline all the vowel plus *r* words they include. Then share stories with the class.

Computer-based Reinforcement   Give students additional practice with *r*-controlled vowel review on *ETC Online,* Units 6.5.2 to 6.5.7.

Lesson 6
igh words

Quick Review

Give students three notecards each and have them write one of the following on each card: *ar, or, er.* Ask them to listen for /är/, /ôr/, and /er/ as you say a list of words. For each word, they should hold up the card for the sound they hear. Word list: *part, port, pert, park, pork, perk, stark, stork, serve, carve, cork, cart, barn, born, swerve.*

Phonemic Awareness

Contrasting Vowel Sounds   Tell students that you are going to say some words that have a short *i* vowel sound, as in *lick,* or a long *i* vowel sound, as in *like.* When they hear a short *i* word they should *pick up* (emphasize the short *i* in *pick*) their pencils, and when they hear a long *i* word they should pretend to *fly* (emphasize the long *i* in *fly*). Words: *by, bit, sit, sight, flight, flip, grime, grin, mind, might.*

Phonics

Introduce the Skill   Write the words *my, mine,* and *mind* on the board. Have students say the words and tell you what kind of vowel is in each (long *i*). Tell students that in this lesson they are going to learn another way to spell the long *i* sound.

Write *might* on the board and pronounce it. Then say the word slowly, drawing out each sound as you point to the letters. Have students show thumbs up or thumbs down to indicate if they hear that letter in the word. As they signal yes for *m, i,* and *t,* underline those letters. Explain that when the letters *igh* come together, the *g* and *h* are silent and the only sound you hear is long *i.* Write *night, sigh, bright,* and *high* on the board. Have volunteers come up to the board, circle the *igh,* and read the word.

Vocabulary

Introduce New Vocabulary   If students are unfamiliar with lesson words or concepts, provide explanations: A king or queen can be called Your **Highness**. At **twilight**, it is getting dark outside. An **acrobat** is a type of circus performer. A **tightrope** is a rope stretched out high in the air that acrobats walk on. A **steeple** is a pointy tower on a building.

Introduce Sight Words   Introduce the new sight word used in the lesson: *sometimes.* Have students make up sentences using the word. Then ask the class to repeat the sight word and spell it aloud. Have them write the letters in the air using their fingers as a pencil. Add this word to the Word Wall or have students add it to their personal dictionaries.

Completing Student Pages 41–48

For each page, read the directions and complete a sample item with students. Identify any pictures that may be unfamiliar, such as *knit* in item 2, being up *high* in the mountains in item 3, using eyes for *sight* in item 4, the *bride* in item 5, a rope *tight* around a tree, and *pies* in item 7 of page 41. Then have students work independently, providing assistance as needed.

Fluency

Noting Punctuation   Tell students that a comma shows where in a sentence to pause briefly. Have students practice reading aloud completed sentences 5–7 on page 46. Check to see if they are pausing briefly after the commas in the sentences.

Comprehension

Synonyms   Remind students that synonyms are words with the same or similar meanings, such as *big* and *large* or *small* and *tiny*. Have students think of synonyms for each of the words below. Tell them that each synonym should be a word that contains the letters *igh* as long *i*.

1. after sunset (night)
2. sparkling (bright)
3. scare (frighten)

4. correct (right)
5. airplane ride (flight)
6. battle (fight)

Writing   Have students write a short rhyme about the *night*, the *bright* sun, being *high* up on a hill, or a pretty *sight*. Encourage them to look through the lesson for other *igh* words to use.

Differentiating Instruction

Learning Styles (Auditory)   Auditory learners may enjoy reciting the following familiar rhyme. Write it on the board and have students underline the *igh* words.

Star light, star bright,
First star I see tonight,
I wish I may, I wish I might
Have the wish I wish tonight.

Encourage them to think of a new verse that also includes *igh* words or other words that rhyme with *light.*

ELL   Some English-language learners may be confused by the concept of silent consonants. Have them write a list of *igh* words from the lesson in two colors, using a lighter color for the *g* and *h* in each word, as a reminder that these letters are not pronounced when the word is said aloud.

Challenge   Point out that some words in English have more than one meaning and that sometimes those meanings are quite different. Use *light* (meaning the opposite of dark or the opposite of heavy) and *right* (as a direction or as a word meaning "correct") as examples of multiple-meaning words. Have students come up with sentences using the two meanings of *light* and *right.* Then have them think of other words that can have two very different meanings, and create sentence pairs for these words.

Computer-based Reinforcement   Give students additional practice with *igh* words on *ETC Online,* Units 6.6.2 to 6.6.7.

Lesson 7

oo words

Quick Review

Ask students to recall how to spell the word *high* and write the word on the board as they spell it for you. Have them tell you what vowel sound the letters *igh* stand for (long *i*) and which letters are silent (*gh*). Elicit other words that contain *igh* and list them on the board.

Phonemic Awareness

Matching Sounds   Tell students to listen as you say groups of three words. Then have them identify the word whose vowel sound is different from the others. As you say each word in the set, emphasize its vowel sound. Model an example: toot, root, nice (nice)

cut, pup, cool (cool)
broke, brook, rope (brook)
loose, lot, lock (loose)
mood, moose, mop (mop)

spun, sun, spoon (spoon)
loose, look, goose (look)
tame, foot, game (foot)

Phonics

Introduce the Skill   Bring in or draw pictures of a book and a boot. Have students identify each item, and write its name as a column head on the board. Underline the *oo* in each word, and point out that *oo* makes different sounds in different words. Slowly say each word, drawing out the vowel sound, and have students repeat the words. Explain to students that when they see a new word that contains *oo,* they should try both pronunciations to see which makes a word they recognize.

Then list some *oo* words along the side of the board; examples include *stool, goose, cook, soon, foot, shook.* Say each one, and have students decide whether the *oo* in the word is the same as in *book* or *boot.* Ask a volunteer to write each word in the correct column.

Vocabulary

Introduce New Vocabulary   If students are unfamiliar with lesson words or concepts, provide explanations: **Soot** is the black dust that comes from fires. A **groom** is a man who is about to be or has just gotten married.

Introduce Sight Words   Introduce the new sight words used in the lesson: *very* and *some.* Have students make up sentences using each word. Then ask the class to repeat the sight words and spell them aloud. Have them write the letters in the air using their fingers as a pencil. Add these words to the Word Wall or have students add the words to their personal dictionaries.

Completing Student Pages 49–56

For each page, read the directions and complete a sample item with students. Identify any pictures that may be unfamiliar: *fist* in item 1, *crook* and *crack* in item 2, *roast* and *raft* in item 6 of page 49. Then have students complete the pages independently, providing assistance as needed.

Fluency

Varying Pitch and Volume   Copy expressive sentences from page 55 on the board, such as the second sentences of numbers 4, 5, 6, and 7. Remind students to read with expression by changing the volume (loudness) and pitch (high and low sounds) of their voices as they read aloud. Read the sentences with appropriate expression then have students practice saying each one, using your reading as a model. Check to see that they are varying their pitch and volume as they speak.

Comprehension

On the board, list three phrases that include words from the lesson: *a **spooky room**, **cooking good food**, a **foolish crook**.* Have students draw and label a sketch that illustrates each phrase.

Writing   Ask students to think of a favorite book they think others would enjoy. Have them write a book report entitled "A Cool Book" to "sell" the book, telling why they like it. Encourage them to include other *oo* words in their report.

Differentiating Instruction
Learning Styles (Auditory)   As you work with auditory learners, precede each sentence with the appropriate pronunciation of the exclamation *Oops!* Pronounce it with the *oo* sound in *book* when focusing on /ŏŏ/ words, and with the *oo* sound in *boot* when focusing on /o͞o/ words. For example:

  Oops! I put the *cookbook* on my *foot!* [pronounce "oops" with the short sound]
  Oops! The *foolish goose* is *loose!* [pronounce "oops" with the long sound]

Work with students to make additional sentences, preceding each one with an appropriately pronounced *Oops!*

ELL   The o͝o sound does not exist in languages including Spanish, Hmong, and Haitian Creole. Give students additional practice with this sound. Have them repeat the following sentences: *The **cook stood** up and put the **cookbook** on the **bookshelf.**/**Look!** His **foot shook** in the chilly **brook.***

Challenge   Remind students that a compound word is made up of two smaller words that often point to the word's meaning. Direct them to list all compounds and their definitions from the lesson, using a dictionary if necessary. You may want to challenge students to create and illustrate "new" compound words that use smaller *oo* words from the lesson, such as *moonfoot* and *woodfood.*

Computer-based Reinforcement   Give students additional practice with *oo* words on *ETC Online,* Units 6.7.2 to 6.7.7.

Lesson 8
ea words

Link to Prior Knowledge
Recall with students that in Book 3 they learned the letters *ea* can spell the long *e* sound. Write the word *eat* on the board and have students read it. Elicit other words that fit this pattern, such as *beat, dream, mean, heat, least,* and *steal.* Tell students that in this lesson they will learn another sound that *ea* can make.

Phonemic Awareness
Contrasting Vowel Sounds   Tell students that you are going to say some words that have a short *e* sound, as in *met,* or a long *e* sound, as in *meet.* Have students stand up. When they hear a short *e* word they should put their hands on the *head* (emphasize the short *e* sound in *head*), and when they hear a long *e* word they should touch their *feet* (emphasize the long *e* sound in *feet*). Words: *men, mean, creep, crept, dead, deal, when, week, health, eat.*

Phonics
Introduce the Skill   Fan yourself with your hand and have students finish this sentence: "Can you feel the (blank)?" (heat). Have students tell you how to spell *heat* and write it on the board. Ask them whether the *ea* in *heat* stands for the long *e* sound or the short *e* sound (long *e*).

     Now take off the *h* and add *sw* to *heat* to make *sweat.* Wipe your brow as you point to the word. Have students finish this sentence: "When I get hot, I begin to (blank)" (sweat).

Ask students if the *ea* in *sweat* stands for the long *e* or the short *e* sound (short *e*). Point out that *ea* can spell either the long *e* or the short *e* sound.

Make two columns headed by *heat* and *sweat*. Now spell aloud each word you used in the phonemic awareness activity. Have students tell you if each is an *ea* word, and if so, in which column it belongs.

Vocabulary

Introduce New Words   If students are unfamiliar with lesson words or concepts, provide explanations: A **billfold**, or wallet, is used to carry money. Children who are running around playing are **romping**. A **meadow** is a field. **Wealth** means having a lot of money.

Introduce Sight Words   Introduce the new sight word used in the lesson: *says*. Have students make up sentences using the word. Then ask the class to repeat the sight word and spell it aloud. Have them write the letters in the air using their fingers as a pencil. Add the word to the Word Wall or have students add it to their personal dictionaries.

Completing Student Pages 57–64

For each page, read the directions and complete a sample item with students. Identify any pictures that may be unfamiliar, such as *sweat* on the child in item 3, the *dead* flower in item 5, and the child's icy *breath* in item 7 on page 57, in addition to the *peacock* in line 2 and the boy with *measles* in line 4 on page 61. Then direct students to complete the pages on their own, providing help as needed.

Fluency

Reading Dialogue   Have students silently read page 18 of "What a Scare!" from *Beyond The Code* Book 4. Then have them practice reading dialogue with a partner. They should read the text in unison until they come to quotation marks, then have one read Toby's lines and the other Jake's. Finally, have them reread the passage, switching parts.

Comprehension

Extending Word Knowledge   Have students discuss the answers to the following questions to demonstrate their understanding of lesson words.

1. What kind of things would you like to **eat** at a **feast**?
2. What might you see if you walked through a **meadow**?
3. Describe a scary **beast** you might **dream** about.
4. What kind of **weather** do you like best?
5. What is one thing you can do to stay **healthy**?

Writing   Have students write a story about a *beast* that lives in a *meadow*. Encourage them to refer to pages 57–64 to find *ea* words that they can use in their story.

Differentiating Instruction

Learning Styles (Kinesthetic)   Draw a picture of a head with an ear on the board. Tell students that if they hear a word with *ea* as in *head* they should tap their heads, and if they hear a word with *ea* as in *ear* they should pull their ear. Call out words from the lesson. Have students repeat the words as they make the appropriate signal. Then have them spell the words and tell you in which column they belong.

Extra Support   Provide students with letter tiles or cards for the letters *a, b, d, e, h, r, t.* Have students use their tiles to form the words *ear, eat, beat, heat, hear, bead, bread,* and *breath.* Then ask them to use each word in an oral sentence.

Challenge   Have students who complete the pages without difficulty create a do-it-yourself crossword puzzle. Show students an example of a crossword puzzle grid. Direct students to make a list of words to use, and help them each make a blank crossword grid to fit the words. They should then write clues for the words. Have them switch puzzles with a friend and try to complete it.

Computer-based Reinforcement   Give students additional practice with *ea* words on *ETC Online,* Units 6.8.4 to 6.8.7.

Lesson 9
ie words

Quick Review

Write *ea* on the board and remind students that these letters put together can make two different sounds. Ask students what the two sounds are (long e and short e) and have them provide an example word for each. Begin two lists on the board with these words as column heads. Then read the following words and have students tell you where to list each one and how to spell it: *dream, bread, peach, sweat, dread, ear.*

Phonemic Awareness

Matching Sounds   Tell students to listen as you say groups of three words. Then have them identify the word with a vowel sound that is different from the other two.

die, chief, field (die)	brief, shy, shield (shy)
tie, thief, tried (thief)	pie, feast, lie (feast)
lies, likes, leaves (leaves)	breath, health, believe (believe)

Phonics

Introduce the Skill   Write *ie* on the board. Point out that like *ea,* these letters put together can make two different sounds. Write the word *pie* on the board and provide an example sentence ("I like to eat apple *pie.*") Do the same with *chief* ("The police *chief* came to visit our class.") Have students say the words slowly with you. Ask: "In which word does *ie* make the long *i* sound? (pie) In which word does *ie* make the long *e* sound? (chief)" List other *ie* words, say them aloud, and work with students to sort them into long *i* or long *e* columns. Examples include *die, field, thief, tried, lies, brief.*

Vocabulary

Introduce New Vocabulary   If you are unsure whether students are familiar with certain lesson words or concepts, provide explanations: A **handkerchief** is a tissue made of cloth. A **shield** is a big decorated piece of metal or wood that soldiers used to use to protect themselves. **Grief** is sadness. A **briefcase** is a small suitcase used for work. **Chiefly** means "mostly." If you are **heaving** something, you are throwing it. **Brief** means quick. When a bird **swoops**, it sweeps down from the sky. A **shortstop** is a baseball player who stands between second and third base.

Introduce Sight Words   Introduce the new sight word used in the lesson: *wear.* Have students make up sentences using the word. Then ask the class to repeat the sight word and spell it aloud. Have them write the letters in the air using their fingers as a pencil. Add this word to the Word Wall or have students add it to their personal dictionaries.

Completing Student Pages 65–72

Read the directions with students. Identify any pictures that may be unfamiliar, such as *tie up the gifts* in item 1, *lie in bed* in item 3, *thin* and *think* in item 5, and the *handkerchief* in item 7 on page 65. Together, complete a sample item on each page. Then have students complete the pages independently, providing assistance as needed.

Fluency

Improving Accuracy   Have partners pick three pairs of sentences on page 71 and practice reading them aloud, smoothly and accurately.

Comprehension

Synonyms   Ask students to come up with an *ie* word that is a synonym of the underlined word in each sentence.

   1. The <u>robber</u> stole some cash. (thief)
   2. She told me a <u>fib</u>. (lie)
   3. There is tall grass in the <u>meadow</u>. (field)
   4. We at some yummy apple <u>crusty dessert</u>. (pie)
   5. I swatted at some pesky <u>insects</u>. (flies)
   6. The police <u>leader</u> came to our class. (chief)

Writing   Have students choose one of the following story ideas: a *thief* who tries not to be bad; a *chief* who *cries* all the time; *flies* causing *mischief;* a missing *pie.* Ask them to write a short story using as many *ie* words from the lesson as they can. Remind them that their stories should answer *when, where,* and *why.*

Differentiating Instruction

Learning Styles (Visual)   Invite visual learners to create two word cards for *ie.* On one card they should print the word *pie* in large letters, gluing glitter on the *i* as a visual reminder that *ie* says long *i* in some words. They should make a similar card for *chief,* gluing glitter to the *e* to signal that *ie* stands for the long *e* sound in some words.

Challenge   Have students who complete the pages without difficulty make an *ie, ee, ea, vowel plus e* chart. Model drawing a full-page grid, three spaces by three spaces. Then write the following categories over the horizontal boxes: First Names, Fruits and Desserts, Book Titles. In front of each vertical box write one of these letters: S, P, B. The challenge is to write in the boxes only words with *ie, ee, ea,* or *vowel plus e* that fit the category and begin with the letter designated by the line. For example, a first name beginning with S might be Sheila, Steve, or Sean.

Computer-based Reinforcement   Give students additional practice with *ie* words on *ETC Online,* Units 6.9.2 to 6.9.7.

Lesson 10
Review Lesson

Cumulative Review

Using index cards, show students the letter combinations *ar, or, er, ir, ur, igh, ea, ie, oo.* Ask them to tell you the sound that each letter combination makes. Remind them that the last three (*ea, ie, oo*) have two sounds.

Phonemic Awareness

Sound Substitution   Model how to substitute initial consonant sounds to make new words: "The word is *school* [Emphasize initial consonant sound.] If I change /sk/ to /st/ I get *stool.*"

1. The word is *feather.* Change /f/ to /w/. What do you get? (weather)
2. The word is *sigh.* Change /s/ to /h/. What do you get? (high)
3. The word is *hoods.* Change /h/ to /w/. What do you get? (woods)
4. The word is *shook.* Change /sh/ to /br/. What do you get? (brook)
5. The word is *sight.* Change /s/ to /r/. What do you get? (right)

Phonics

Skill Review   Write the following words in a column on the board: *star, fork, her, bird, burn, light, boot, book, eat, head, pie, chief.* Have the class read the words together. Ask them to copy the words on paper, then write another word beside each that is spelled with the same vowel combination and makes the same sound.

Vocabulary

Introduce New Vocabulary   If students are not familiar with lesson words or concepts, provide explanations: **Snoopy** is the name of a cartoon dog. If you are **stooping**, you are leaning over. When people go **sightseeing**, they visit a place and look around. A **repairer** fixes things. **Breathless** means out of breath.

Introduce Sight Words   Introduce the new sight words used in the lesson: *down* and *said.* Have students make up sentences using each word. Then ask the class to repeat the sight words and spell them aloud. Have them write the letters in the air using their fingers as a pencil. Add these words to the Word Wall or have students add the words to their personal dictionaries.

Completing Student Pages 73–80

For each page, read the directions and complete a sample item with students. Identify any pictures that may be unfamiliar, such as *zipper* and *zoo* in item 2, the *hood* of a car in item 4, the water in a *stream* in item 6, and the child in a *highchair* in item 6 on page 73.

Fluency

Articulation   Have students work with a partner to practice reading aloud their completed sentences on page 76. You might pair a struggling reader with a more fluent reader who can model reading each word clearly and accurately.

Comprehension

Similes   List these words on the board: *feather, sweat, fright, night, pie, field, beast, zoo, shook, foot.* Then write the simile sentences below. Remind students that in a simile, two things are being compared because they are alike in some way. Read each sentence with students and have them choose a word from the list above to complete the simile. Then have students identify the trait the two compared items share (for example, *dark* for "room" and "night" in sentence 1).

   1. Kim's room was as dark as _____. (night)
   2. Even though it is big, this package is as light as a _____. (feather)
   3. Steve felt bad about breaking the glass, and was as sweet as _____ for the rest of the day. (pie)
   4. Our noisy school cafeteria is like a _____ sometimes! (zoo)
   5. Tim was so worried, he _____ like a leaf in the wind. (shook)

Writing   Have students work in pairs to create their own similes. Write the first part on the board. Have students copy them on sheets of paper and fill in the blanks. Examples: *as smooth as* (blank), *as crooked as* (blank), *as bright as* (blank), *as neat as* (blank), *as foolish as* (blank). Share similes with the class.

Differentiating Instruction

Extra Practice   On separate cards write several words that contain the various vowel spellings (*igh, ea, oo,* and *ie*); use words from pages 73–80. Have partners mix up the cards and stack them face down. The first person picks a card and tries to read the word correctly the first time. If he or she is successful the card is kept and the next player chooses a card; if not, the card goes back in the pile. The winner is the one with the most cards.

Challenge   Students who complete these pages without difficulty can write three new similes using any words presented in this lesson. Have them trade papers with a partner, leaving off the comparison word, and have the partners try to fill in the blanks and determine the comparison.

Computer-based Reinforcement   Give students additional practice on *ETC Online,* Units 6.10.2 to 6.10.7.

Lesson 11
oi and *oy* words

Quick Review

Write these words on the board and have students pronounce them: *heat, fright, breath, stood, cried, shield, moon.* Then have volunteers come to the board and circle the letters that make the vowel sounds in each word (*ea, igh, ea, oo, ie, ie, oo*).

Phonemic Awareness

Matching Sounds   Have students listen for the word that contains the *oi* sound as in *boy* as you say each set of three words:

Jay, Joy, Joe (Joy)	point, pint, pant (point)
most, move, moist (moist)	spill, spoil, spool (spoil)
foil, foul, fool (foil)	towing, tooling, toiling (toiling)

Phonics

Introduce the Skill   Remind students that they have learned several ways to spell different vowel sounds. Tell them that in this lesson they will learn two ways to spell a new vowel sound. Write *oi* and *oy* on the board and explain that these sets of letters both stand for /oi/. Ask: "What happens to water when you heat it up?" (it boils) Write *boil* on the board.

Then point to a boy in the class and say, "He's not a puppy dog, he's a (*blank*)." (boy) Write *boy* on the board.

Elicit rhyming words for *boil* and *boy* (*oil, broil, coil, foil, soil; joy, Roy, toy*), listing them on the board under the appropriate word. Read each word aloud and have a volunteer come up to the board and circle the letters that make the *oi* sound in that word.

Vocabulary

Introduce New Words   If you are unsure whether students are familiar with certain lesson words or concepts, provide explanations: A **joint** is a body part that bends, like an elbow or knee. You can **coil** a rope into a neat pile. One way to cook meat is to **broil** it. If you cut yourself, you can put first-aid **ointment**, or cream, on the wound. An **oyster** is a sea animal that lives in a shell. A **pooch** is a dog. If you yell and scream, you are having a **tantrum**, which might **annoy**—or bother—the people around you. **Pavement** is the concrete of a road.

Introduce Sight Words   Introduce the new sight words used in the lesson: *bandage* and *should*. Have students make up sentences using each word. Then ask the class to repeat the sight words and spell them aloud. Have them write the letters in the air using their fingers as a pencil. Add these words to the Word Wall or have students add them to their personal dictionaries.

Completing Student Pages 81–88

For each page, read the directions and work through a sample item with students. Identify any pictures that may be unfamiliar, such as *oilcan* and *joy* in item 4, the bottle of *poison* and the *pond* in item 5, and the pet that did *annoy* its owner in item 7 of page 81, in addition to the two people who *join* hands in item 7 on page 83. Have students complete the pages, providing assistance as needed.

Fluency

Phrasing   Remind students that an important part of reading aloud is being able to read smoothly. When reading a sentence, suggest that they look for words that seem to belong together in a group, rather than reading each word separately. Model reading some of the completed sentences on page 84, paying particular attention to phrasing. Then have students practice reading these sentences aloud.

Comprehension

Word Endings   List these words on the board: *oil, point, annoy*. Then make a separate list of endings: *-s, -ed, -ing, -y*. Have students write each word on a separate card and circle it. Then direct them to complete a word web for each word, making new words by adding as many of the endings as they can to the central word and writing these words around the circle. Students can make *oils, oiled, oiling, oily; points, pointed, pointing, pointy; annoys, annoyed, annoying*. Have them use each word they create in an oral sentence.

Writing   Have students write a story that begins: "What is that *noise*?" Remind them that a story needs to tell *who, what, when, where, how,* and *why* something happened. Encourage them to use as many *oi* and *oy* words as they can. Then share stories with the class.

Differentiating Instruction

Extra Practice   For extra practice with *oi* and *oy,* have students complete the activities in *Explode The Code* Book 6½, Lesson 9.

ELL   The *oi* sound does not exist in all languages. If this sound is unknown to students, lead them in saying *o* and *e* together, faster and faster, to help them gain familiarity with the sound. Then have them practice tongue twisters that contain /oi/ words: *Joy and Roy play with toys. The boy points at the oilcan.*

Challenge   Students who complete these pages without difficulty might enjoy creating /oi/ tongue twisters. Model the classic tongue twister *toy boat* as an example. Remind them that tongue twisters can be whole sentences as well as phrases.

Computer-based Reinforcement   Give students additional practice with *oi* and *oy* words on *ETC Online,* Units 6.11.2 to 6.11.6.

Lesson 12
ou and *ow* words

Link to Prior Knowledge

Write the word *low* on the board and have students read it. Underline the *ow* and remind students that they learned way back in Book 3 that *ow* can make the long *o* sound. Elicit *ow* words by having students guess what word you are pantomiming; for example, *blow* out air and pretend to *throw* a ball. Ask students to spell the words for you as you write them on the board. Tell students that they are going to learn another sound that *ow* can make, as well as another way to spell that same sound.

Phonemic Awareness

Matching Sounds   Direct students to listen as you say a group of three words and to tell you which word contains the sound *ou/ow,* as in *mouse* or *cow.*

polar, paler, power (power)	cleaned, cloud, clad (cloud)
horse, haste, house (house)	frown, free, food (frown)
pound, pinned, paint (pound)	grow, gray, growl (growl)

Phonics

Introduce the Skill   Hold up a picture of a cow, and have students identify it. Then write *cow* on the board, and have students read it with you. Ask students what shape a ball is (round), write the word on the board, and have students read it with you.

Elicit rhyming words for *cow* (*how, now, plow, sow, wow*) and *round* (*found, hound, mound, pound, sound*), and write them on the board. Have students come up and underline the vowel sound in each word. Show how *ow* and *ou* are alike in these words because they make the same vowel sound, but they are spelled differently.

Vocabulary

Introduce New Vocabulary   If students are unfamiliar with lesson words or concepts, provide explanations: A **lighthouse** is a skinny building with a light at the top that helps ships find their way in the dark. Farmers use animals or machines to do **plowing**, digging rows for planting crops. A **flounder** is a type of fish that lives in the ocean. **Drowsy** means "sleepy." A **trout** is a type of fish that lives in streams. A **bulldozer** is a truck that clears land. A rain **shower** is a quick burst of rain. When you take a **bow** you bend over at the waist.

Completing Student Pages 89–96

Review each page with students and read the directions together. Identify any pictures that may be unfamiliar, such as *grab* at the dog's collar in item 4, the *outside* and the *saddle* in item 5, the *nightgown* in item 6, and the *lighthouse* in item 7 of page 89.

Fluency

Noting Punctuation   Remind students that a comma shows where to pause briefly when you read aloud. Have students practice reading the completed sentences 1, 2, and 4 on page 94. Also suggest that they practice reading page 35 of "A Different Kind of Library" from *Beyond The Code* Book 4, noting the commas and periods.

Comprehension

If necessary, explain that a "hink pink" is a silly riddle with an answer made up of two rhyming words. Write this example on the board and read it to students: "What do you call a dirt-colored evening dress?" (brown gown) Have students note that the answer is two /ou/ words that rhyme, and discuss the answer to make sure students understand why it fits the riddle. Then have students solve the following hink pinks. If they have any trouble, provide the first word of the answer.

1. What do you call a tall building covered with roses? (flower tower)
2. What do you call a sofa that makes you shout, "Ow!"? (ouch couch)
3. What do you call a nasty nighttime bird? (foul owl)
4. What do you call a noisy, fluffy thing in the sky? (loud cloud)
5. What do you call a village full of circus performers who make you laugh? (Clown Town)
6. What is a small rodent that likes to stay inside a home? (house mouse)

Writing   Invite students to write a story about one of the hink pinks, using some other /ou/ words from the lesson.

Differentiating Instruction

Learning Styles (Visual) Have visual learners draw and label a picture of a snowplow with *ow* on its side, to remind them of the two sounds that *ow* can stand for.

Extra Practice For extra practice with *ou* and *ow*, have students complete the activities in *Explode The Code* Book 6½, Lesson 10.

Challenge Ask students to name the two sounds of *ow*. Then list these words: *bow, row, tower,* and *shower.* Some are pronounced two ways; some are not. For each one, have students list two meanings, using a dictionary as needed. Challenge them to write a sentence for each word.

Computer-based Reinforcement Give students additional practice with *ou* and *ow* words on *ETC Online,* Units 6.12.2 to 6.12.7.

Lesson 13
au and *aw* words

Quick Review

Moo like a cow and have students tell you what animal you are imitating. Ask them to spell *cow* for you as you write it on the board. Then point to your mouth and have students tell you the word. Have them spell *mouth* as you write it on the board. Underline *ow* in *cow* and *ou* in *mouth;* ask students what sound these letter pairs make (/ou/). Then have students name other /ou/ words. Work together to spell them, listing *ow* words under *cow* and *ou* words under *mouth.*

Phonemic Awareness

Matching Sounds Direct students to listen as you say a group of three words and to tell you which word contains the sound *aw/au,* as in *saw* or *haul.*

draw, dream, drain (draw)
cool, kite, caught (caught)
straw, strew, stray (straw)

hunt, haunt, hint (haunt)
jaw, Joy, jump (jaw)

Phonics

Introduce the Skill Explain to students that they will be working with a new vowel sound and two ways to spell that sound. Write *au* and *aw* on the board, and tell students that both of these letter pairs say /aw/ as in *saw.*

Ask students what month comes before September (August); write it under *au.* Have students say *August,* underlining the *Au.* Then yawn and have students tell you what you just did. Write *yawn* on the board, have students say it, and underline *aw.* Have students tell you how *au* and *aw* are alike (they make the same sound) and different (they are spelled differently).

Ask students to think of other words that contain the *au/aw* sound, including people's names (Paul, Audrey, Dawn, Shawn, Laura). Orally spell each word and have students tell you where to list it. When the lists are complete, have students come up and underline the *au/aw* sound in each word as the class says it.

Vocabulary

Introduce New Vocabulary   If students are unfamiliar with lesson words or concepts, provide explanations: You can put a **shawl** over your shoulders to stay warm. An **auto** is a car. An athlete uses a long rod to **polevault** over a very high bar. **Coleslaw** is a salad made of cabbage and mayonnaise. If you run and fall, you may go **sprawling**. When something frozen gets warmer, it is **thawing**. A **lumberjack** cuts down trees. **Autumn** is the season also known as fall. If you feel **awkward**, you feel uncomfortable.

Completing Student Pages 97–104

For each page, read the directions and complete a sample item with students. Identify any pictures that may be unfamiliar, such as *pay* in item 1, *jaw* in item 4, *yawn* in item 6, *clam* and *claw* in item 7 of page 97. Then direct students to complete the pages on their own, providing assistance as needed.

Fluency

Improving Accuracy   Assign partners and have them read the sentence pairs on page 103, monitoring each other for accuracy. Also have partners practice reading "Am I a Water Buffalo?" on page 90 of *Beyond The Code* Book 4 until they can read the paragraph smoothly and easily.

Comprehension

Have students discuss their responses to the following prompts, to demonstrate their understanding of lesson words:

1. Which animal is more scary: a **fawn** or a **hawk**?
2. Which chore would you rather do: **haul autumn** leaves or mow the **lawn**?
3. Name a time when you felt **awkward** and **awful**.
4. Name some animals that have **paws** and **claws**.
5. Name your favorite **author**.

Writing   Write these phrases on the board: *clean **laundry**, an **awkward fawn**, a **hawk** with sharp **claws**, **autumn leaves**.* Have students write *when* or *where* sentences including each of the phrases, and draw accompanying pictures for each.

Differentiating Instruction

Learning Styles (Auditory)   For auditory learners, point out that *aw!* is an interjection, something people say with feeling, like *ouch!* and *eek!* Have students take turns pointing to the picture that matches each word on page 97 and identifying it, using this frame: "Aw-w-w-w! It's a picture of a (*blank*)!" Suggest they use this interjection to remind themselves of the sound made by *au* and *aw*.

Extra Practice   For extra practice with *au* and *aw*, have students complete the exercises in *Explode The Code* Book 6½, Lesson 11.

Challenge   Have students who complete these pages without difficulty write six questions like those on page 100, using at least one *au* or *aw* word in each. Then have them trade papers with another challenger and answer each other's questions.

Computer-based Reinforcement   Give students additional practice with *au* and *aw* words on *ETC Online*, Units 6.13.2 to 6.13.7.

Lesson 14

ew, ue, ui, and *ou* words

Link to Prior Knowledge

Draw a picture of a boot on the board. Have students identify and spell the word *boot* as you write it on the board. Underline the *oo* and ask students to tell you the vowel sound in *boot* (/o͞o/). Tell students that in this lesson they will learn some other ways to spell the o͞o sound.

Phonemic Awareness

Sound Substitution   Model how to substitute initial consonant sounds to make new words: "The word is *tuned.* [Emphasize initial consonant sound.] If I change /t/ to /w/, I get *wound.*" Have students do the following:

1. The word is *soup.* Change /s/ to /gr/. What do you get? (group)
2. The word is *stew.* Change /st/ to /ch/. What do you get? (chew)
3. The word is *blue.* Change /bl/ to /gl/. What do you get? (glue)
4. The word is *suit.* Change /s/ to /fr/. What do you get? (fruit)
5. The word is *grew.* Change /g/ to /th/. What do you get? (threw)
6. The word is *lose.* Change /l/ to /n/. What do you get? (news)

Phonics

Introduce the Skill   Write *ue, ui, ew,* and *ou* on the board. Point to the first three and explain that each of these combinations says (/o͞o/). Point to *ou* and have students recall what *sound* (emphasize the word) they have learned for *ou* (/ou/ as in *sound*). Explain that sometimes *ou* makes the o͞o sound.

Point to something blue and have students identify the color. Spell *blue* orally and have students tell you where to list it (under *ue*). Follow the same procedure with these words: *fruit* (hold up or draw two pieces of fruit), *screw* (hold up or draw a screw), and *soup* (hold up or draw a soup can). Afterward, have students read each word as a volunteer underlines the two letters that spell the o͞o sound.

Vocabulary

Introduce New Vocabulary   If students are unfamiliar with lesson words or concepts, provide explanations: A boat may **cruise** slowly through the water. A marble **statue** is a carving made from hard white stone. **Drapes** are curtains.

Completing Student Pages 105–110

For each page, read the directions and complete a sample item with students. Identify any pictures that may be unfamiliar, such as the *flute* in item 1, the *glue* and the flower that *grew* in item 2, the *soap* in item 5, and the *new* dress in item 6 on page 105. Also note *chew* in item 6 on page 107 and the *scarecrow* at the bottom of page 109. Then have students complete the pages independently, providing assistance as needed.

Fluency

Noting Punctuation   Remind students that a comma shows them where to pause briefly when they are reading aloud. Also remind them to note question marks and to raise their voices as they read questions. Then have students practice reading their completed sentences on page 110, noting commas and question marks. You may also suggest that they practice reading "The Treasure Hunt" on page 75 of *Beyond The Code* Book 4, paying careful attention to proper punctuation.

Comprehension

Tell students that the answer to each riddle below includes at least one /o͞o/ word from their lesson. Discuss the answers, including any that involve a play on words with different spellings (*read/red, chew-chew/choo-choo, overdue/over dew*).

1. What's black and white and red all over? (a *newspaper,* because it is read all over)
2. What kind of clothes could you get when you buy a deck of cards? (four *suits,* because there are four suits in a deck of cards)
3. What bird is always sad? (a *blue* jay; its color is *blue* and it is *blue* meaning *sad*)
4. What do you call a train that eats everything in sight? (a *chew-chew/choo-choo*)
5. How is a late library book like a bee flying over moist grass? (They're both *overdue/over dew.*)

Writing Have students create a book of riddles that includes the five riddles above as well as some of their own favorite riddles. Each page should have the riddle and an illustration on one side, and the answer on the reverse side.

Differentiating Instruction

Learning Styles (Visual) Have visual learners create a six-sided cube from construction paper. On one side, they should write o͞o in one color. On the other sides, in a different color, they write the four spellings for /o͞o/ they've just learned (*ew, ue, ui, ou*), as well as *oo*. Suggest they write a key word for each spelling (*suit, blue, new, group, boot*) and keep their o͞o square handy to remind them of the different spellings.

Extra Practice For extra practice with *ew, ue, ui,* and *ou*, have students complete the exercises in *Explode The Code*, Book 6½, Lesson 12.

Challenge Any students who complete the pages without difficulty may enjoy playing with /o͞o/ homophones. Have them find two words in the lesson that sound the same but are spelled differently (*blew/blue*). Then have them brainstorm homophones for *dew (due, do), cruise (crews), bruise (brews), new (knew, gnu), flew (flu, flue),* and *threw (through)*.

Computer-based Reinforcement Give students additional practice with *ew, ui, ue,* and *ou* words on *ETC Online,* Units 6.14.2 to 6.14.7.

Lesson 15
Review Lesson

Cumulative Review

Remind students that they have been learning several ways to spell different vowel sounds. List the key words from each lesson (for example, *star* in Lesson 1 and *fork* in Lesson 2). For Lesson 15 (key word *suit*), add *new, blue,* and *soup.* Keep this list on the board throughout the review lesson.

For each word listed, have students read the whole word and then isolate the vowel sound. Next, have a volunteer underline the letters that spell this vowel sound. For example, students would say *star* and /är/, and the volunteer would underline *ar*.

Phonemic Awareness

Matching Sounds Tell students that you will say sets of three words, two of which share the same vowel sound. Have students tell you which word contains a different vowel sound. Model this for students with the first item.

sweat, sore, swarm (sweat)	light, lie, law (law)
ground, group, growl (group)	fern, farm, fur (farm)
book, boil, boy (book)	world, swirl, suit (suit)

Phonics

Skill Review   Have students suggest an additional word that shares the same vowel sound/spelling with each key word on the board. Ask volunteers to come to the board to spell this word, or have the group dictate its spelling to the volunteer.

Help students make connections among the various letter sounds/spellings they have learned in Book 6, using the list of key words generated in the Cumulative Review activity. Begin by having students look for key words that share the same vowel sound (for example, *light* and *pie*). Help them sort the key words by vowel sounds to see which letter combinations can stand for the same sound (*er/ir/ur, ie/ea, ie/light, ou/ow, oi/oy, au/aw, oo/ew/ui/ue/ou*).

Then focus on each letter combination that can stand for different sounds in different words (*ou* as /ou/ or /o͞o/, *ea* as /ĕ/ or /ē/, *ie* as /ē/ or /ī/, and *oo* as /o͝o/ or /o͞o/). Help students pull out key words that share vowel-sound spellings. Work with them to sort these words, first by vowel spellings (for example, *eat* and *head*) and then by vowel sounds (*eat* and *chief*).

Vocabulary

Introduce New Words   If students are unfamiliar with lesson words or concepts, provide explanations: A **trombone** is a kind of musical instrument. A **jigsaw** is a puzzle but a **hacksaw** is a tool. A **caboose** is the last car of a train. A **bluebell** is a type of flower. To **saunter** means to walk slowly. A **prowler** is someone who walks around in a mysterious way. A **flounder** is a kind of fish. A **countdown** is counting backwards to zero.

Introduce Sight Words   Introduce the new sight words used in the lesson: *friend, wash,* and *lives.* Have students make up sentences using each word. Then ask the class to repeat the sight words and spell them aloud. Have them write the letters in the air using their fingers as a pencil. Add these words to the Word Wall or have students add the words to their personal dictionaries.

Completing Student Pages 113–120

Read the directions with students. Identify any pictures that may be unfamiliar, such as *wishbone* and *handstand* in item 1, *baboon* in item 4, the pile of *sawdust* in item 5, and the *jewel* in item 6 on page 113, in addition to the *pretzel* in item 6 on page 115. Then have students complete the pages independently, providing assistance as needed.

Fluency

Improving Rate   Have students chorally read the completed sentences on page 118. Guide them to set a pace that moves smoothly along but still allows them time to pronounce the words clearly and accurately. Then as a group, reread students' favorite sentences at a slightly faster pace.

Comprehension

On separate cards, write some words from each of the lessons in Book 6. Have students pick two cards without looking at them and then make up an oral sentence using these two words. Repeat until all cards have been selected.

Writing   Write the following sentence on the board and ask students to write a story using it as a story starter: *As I was digging in my garden, I was surprised to find a buried suitcase . . .* Remind them to include details telling what happened and why, to make their stories more interesting. Encourage them to use as many words they learned in Book 6 as possible; you could offer a prize to the student who uses the most words in a way that makes sense.

Differentiating Instruction

Extra Practice   Provide cards with many of the lesson words covered in Book 6. Have students sort the words into piles based on the sound–symbol categories they have learned. They should then read each word and use it in an oral sentence.

Challenge   Challenge students who complete these pages without difficulty to write as many words that include the base words *light* and *count* as they can. Remind them to add letters at the beginning and/or end, and make two- and three-syllable words as well. Answers include: *lightning, flashlight, delight, flight, lighthouse and counter, recount, countess, countless, countertop, discount.* Give clues if necessary.

Computer-based Reinforcement   Give students additional practice on *ETC Online*, Units 6.15.2 to 6.15.7.

Book 6 Posttest Pages 121–124

You may wish to have students complete the pages of the posttest in more than one sitting. Read each set of directions with students. Observe as students begin working independently to be sure they understand how to complete each page. Introduce the sight word *early*.

Page 121. Students circle the two words in each group with the same vowel sound. These words are:

1. frown/couch; 2. field/teach; 3. blest/spread; 4. glide/slight; 5. moist/oyster;
6. churn/third; 7. stoop/flew; 8. shows/groans; 9. world/churn; 10. chain/paste;
11. fault/drawn; 12. fruit/gloom

Page 122. Give the instruction "Circle the word you hear," and dictate the words listed below. Students then circle the correct word from a choice of five words.

1. squirming; 2. sprawling; 3. powdery; 4. chiefly; 5. frightening; 6. withdrew;
7. northeaster; 8. pleasant; 9. harpooned; 10. understood

Page 123. Students write sentences dictated by the teacher. Dictate each sentence slowly once or twice. It is often helpful for the students to repeat the sentence before they write it.

1. The stars and the moon shine at night.
2. You can use a straw to sip a milkshake.
3. A storm from the north may blow hard.
4. I can see my footprints in the sawdust.
5. Pork chops smell good when Mom broils them.
6. A toothbrush helps to make your mouth clean.

Page 124. Students complete this page on their own. Simple directions are included at the top of the Posttest. Students read short paragraphs and select the words that best complete the sentences. These words are:

1. moonlit, surf, foot, shark, beach
2. warning, outdoors, lightning, burning, fireworks
3. worms, sneakers, barefoot, trout, threw, raccoon

Book 6½ Posttest Pages 105–108

Page 105. Students circle the two words in each group with the same vowel sound. These words are:

1. balloon/glue; 2. beach/steam; 3. cry/flight; 4. warmth/storm; 5. caught/yawn;
6. roast/most; 7. count/scout; 8. learn/burnt; 9. point/boy; 10. word/purse; 11. thirst/hurt;
12. steak/break

Page 106. Give the instruction "Circle the word you hear," and dictate the words listed below. Students then circle the correct word from a choice of five words.

1. unearthed; 2. worst; 3. heavy; 4. fielder; 5. rousted; 6. threw; 7. lightest; 8. believe; 9. couches; 10. sprouted

Page 107. Students write sentences dictated by the teacher. Dictate each sentence slowly once or twice. It is often helpful for the students to repeat the sentence before they write it.

1. The carpenter is pointing to her wooden toolbox.
2. Which person threw the old newspapers out?
3. The outlaw hauled the highchair into the tower.
4. The hockey team met at the field for a workout.
5. How did you learn to count by tens?

Page 108. Students complete this page on their own. Simple directions are included at the top of the Posttest. Students read short paragraphs and select the words that best complete the sentences. These words are:

1. newspaper, break, underneath, auto, looking, outlaws, highway, warned, report
2. jockey, shorter, heavy, pounds, horseback, high, willpower, thousand, worthwhile
3. fireworks, ballfield, pointed, backward, brightest, loudest

Posttest Scores

- **80% items correct:** Mastery of skills presented in Book 6. Have students begin work in Book 8.
- **Less than 80% items correct:** Review skills in Book 6 as needed.